CASSELL'S GARDEN DIRECTORIES

The Wild Garden

CASSELL'S GARDEN DIRECTORIES

The Wild Garden

EVERYTHING YOU NEED TO CREATE A GARDEN

LUCY HUNTINGTON

CASSELL&CO

First published in the United Kingdom in 2002 by CASSELL & CO

Design and text copyright © The Ivy Press Limited 2000

A CIP Catalogue record for this book
is available from the British Library

ISBN 0 304 36232 8

This book was conceived,
designed and produced by
THE IVY PRESS LIMITED
The Old Candlemakers, West Street,
Lewes, East Sussex BN7 2NZ

Creative Director: PETER BRIDGEWATER
Designers: AXIS DESIGN
Editorial Director: SOPHIE COLLINS
Project Editor: ANDREW KIRK
Illustrations: VANESSA LUFF & PETER BULL
Picture Researcher: LIZ EDDISON

Originated and printed in China by
Hong Kong Graphics and Printing Ltd

This book is typeset in 10.5/13 Linotype Perpetua and Univers

CASSELL & CO.
Wellington House, 125 Strand, London WC2R 0BB

CONTENTS

INTRODUCTION

There has always been wildlife in gardens: bees, butterflies and birds have been constant visitors since people first planted gardens, and ants and earthworms, centipedes and beetles have never stopped working away in the soil and leaf debris beneath our feet. In the past, we did not consider them when planning and planting gardens, but simply left them to their own devices as long as they did not damage our plants. The difference now is that we are beginning to realize the significance of sharing our outside space with these creatures and that we need to understand their way of life and to encourage them to flourish.

Until quite recently, most gardens were areas from which all wild animals were rigorously excluded. Walls and fences were erected around the garden to keep out deer and rabbits, which might get in and eat the roses and lettuces. Fruit cages and netting kept birds off fruits such as raspberries and strawberries. Mole traps were set to prevent mole hills destroying the lawn, and squirrel traps tried to prevent these invaders from damaging our trees. All insect pests, including greenfly, blackfly and weevils, were sprayed with insecticides to prevent them damaging our flowers. All in all, gardens were places for ornamental plants and flowers in weed-free beds, with close-cut lawns and perfect rows of cabbages unsullied by caterpillars.

That is now changing, and many gardeners are now seeing their gardens as important refuges for many mammals, amphibians, birds, bees and butterflies, which see their native habitats disappearing with the spread of urban development and intensive farming practices.

HINTS AND TIPS

Some of the following types of wildlife and wild plants can usually be tempted into the garden, whatever its size.
- Small mammals, including squirrels, hedgehogs and voles.
- Many types of birds, from wrens and robins to fieldfares.
- A huge number of insects, the most obvious and attractive being butterflies, dragonflies, honeybees and bumblebees.
- Plants that are native to your area, that is, those that may be found growing wild, such as in wildflower meadows.

WELCOMING WILDLIFE

Creating a garden for wildlife does require a new approach to gardening, a more organic approach, as we allow nature to arrive at a balance. If we stop spraying the greenfly in order not to kill the bees, then we must encourage the ladybirds who naturally eat the greenfly. If we want to have beautiful butterflies flitting over our flower borders, then we will have to accept their caterpillars eating the leaves of our violets and cabbages. If we want the sound and movement of birds as they gather berries from our shrubs, then we will have to be prepared to net our vegetables against pigeons and accept the occasional ravages of bullfinches on our blossoming trees.

As well as being a refuge for native fauna, gardens are now becoming a last resort for many of the wild flowers threatened with extinction in the countryside. The corn cockle, a pretty pink flower of cornfields, had almost disappeared owing to the use of herbicides by farmers, but is

LEFT *Honeybees visit flowers for both pollen and nectar, which they turn into honey.* *In so doing, they carry pollen from one flower to another, helping the plant to reproduce.*

now finding a new habitat as part of gardens. The advantage of including wild flowers such as the corn cockle is that so many of them are rich sources of nectar and pollen for bees, butterflies and other insects as well as being very important food plants for caterpillars.

Whether your garden is a small paved town garden or a large country garden surrounded by fields, there should always be room for some elements of the native fauna and flora. In return for welcoming wildlife into your garden, you will be rewarded by the pleasure of watching and learning from these new inhabitants. You can observe the dancing patterns of bees collecting pollen and nectar, watch the miracle of a butterfly emerging from its chrysalis, or follow the development of frogspawn into tiny tadpoles and then into frogs. Almost everyone enjoys the patient

ABOVE *A wildflower border will not only look stunning in the height of summer but also act as a magnet for many kinds of insects, including a selection of attractive butterflies.*

robin waiting to grab an earthworm as we dig our beds in spring, or the translucent wings of a dragonfly as it hovers over the pond. Children can spend hours lying in a wildflower meadow, watching the various insects busy working among the wide variety of plants.

A garden planned and planted with wildlife in mind can still be a beautiful garden – although perhaps not as perfect as a garden rigorously controlled by insecticides and pesticides – but at the same time it will be full of life and sound and movement, gently humming with activity and in peace and harmony with its surroundings.

HOW TO USE THIS BOOK

Cassell's Garden Directories have been conceived and written to appeal both to gardening beginners and to confident gardeners who need advice for a specific project. Each book focuses on a particular type of garden, drawing on the experience of an established expert. The emphasis is on a practical and down-to-earth approach that takes account of the space, time and money that you have available. The ideas and techniques in these books will help you to produce an attractive and manageable garden that you will enjoy for years to come.

The Wild Garden takes as its starting point one of the most attractive aspects of gardening, the joy of watching wildlife in your very own garden. The book is divided into three sections. The opening section, Planning Your Garden, introduces the subject of gardening for wildlife, looking at different habitats and the range of native plants that is available. There are also three specific inspirational garden plans for producing a really wild garden, a suburban retreat and an urban oasis.

Part Two of the book, Creating Your Garden, moves on to the practicalities of buying and planting appropriate plants. This section opens with some advice on the range of different birds, insects and pond life you may wish to attract. It continues with tips on controlling pests and diseases, and shows how to re-create different types of habitat, such as woodland margins, hedgerows, meadows and wetlands. Flower borders, herb gardens, secret places and the wild garden at night are also covered here.

This section is packed with practical information on basic techniques such as sowing, feeding and weeding plants, dividing seedlings, and supporting and pruning plants. Moving on from this basic grounding, this section then encourages you to put your skills to work with a series of specific projects such as sowing a wildflower cornfield and planting a mixed native hedge. There are step-by-step illustrations throughout this section that show clearly and simply what you need to do to achieve the best results. Also included are handy hints and tips, points to watch out for, and star plants that are particularly suitable for the projects that are described.

The final part of the book, The Plant Directory, is a comprehensive listing of all the plants mentioned in the earlier sections, together with other plants that will bring wildlife to your garden. Each plant is illustrated, and there is complete information on appropriate growing conditions, speed of growth and ease of maintenance.

GARDEN SCHEMES are included to inspire you to great things in your own garden.

COLOUR PHOTOGRAPHS show what can be achieved with a little effort and imagination.

3D PLANS show the best planting scheme for you to achieve the right effect.

THE KEY FEATURES of each part of the garden are described to help you visualize the plan.

CHOICES SPREADS show the range of wildlife that can be encouraged to come into your garden.

COLOUR PHOTOGRAPHS help you to identify the wildlife that you may find in your garden.

THE CHECKLIST lists plants that particular birds, animals or insects will find attractive.

CLEAR ILLUSTRATIONS show each step of the process.

PRACTICAL SPREADS give useful information on basic techniques and garden projects.

THE PLANT DIRECTORY is organized into categories making it simple to find a particular type of plant.

CLEAR DESCRIPTIVE TEXT details the appearance and the appropriate growing conditions for each plant.

THE SYMBOLS PANEL gives important information on features such as speed of growth and shade-tolerance.

COLOUR PHOTOGRAPHS clearly identify each plant listed.

SIDEBAR shows at a glance the season of interest for each plant.

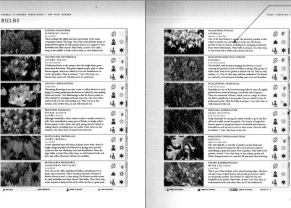

PLANNING YOUR GARDEN

1

Although the finished result should look completely natural, a wildlife garden requires a great deal of thought in the planning stages in order to get the balance of planting just right. You will need to consider whether you are trying to recreate a specific type of habitat in your garden, or in one part of it, or whether you just want to provide the best conditions throughout the garden for wildlife to thrive. This section is full of ideas to suit any size and type of garden.

LEFT *In gardens, a profusion of bright seasonal flowers like this does not just happen – your wild garden will benefit from meticulous planning.*

WHAT IS A WILDLIFE GARDEN?

Any garden could be considered as a wildlife garden of sorts — after all, no garden could claim to be insect-free, and all gardeners welcome the invaluable earthworm. The difference is that in a true wildlife garden people actually wish to encourage insects, even if some of them may cause damage to the occasional flower, and will be happy to see wild poppies coming up in the middle of flowerbeds and borders.

Why on earth would any gardener want a wildlife garden? After all, most gardeners spend a great deal of time, effort and money keeping wildlife such as rabbits, pigeons and cabbage-white caterpillars out of the garden. Some gardeners would also include bullfinches, squirrels, moles, greenfly, blackfly, codlin moth, eelworms and even badgers and foxes in the list of unwanted guests.

In the past, gardeners did not consider wildlife as something to be welcomed into the garden, and tentative gestures at growing wild flowers, including naturalizing daffodils in the lawn or planting a wildflower meadow in an attempt to re-create a half-remembered idyll of child-hood hayfields rich in a colourful tapestry of cowslips, pink campion and ox-eye daisies, were the exception to the rule.

THEN AND NOW

✿ In the past, gardens were places for cultivated plants to be grown, and all animals and weeds were kept well away by every possible means.

✿ Now gardens are seen as part of an important resource of potential habitats for native wild plants and animals.

SILENT SPRING

One of the major catalysts for change was the publication of the book *Silent Spring* by Rachel Carson in the early 1960s. This book drew attention to the damage farmers were doing to wildlife through their increasing use of chemicals. It also enumerated the reduction of habitats by increased mechanization, including the removal of hedgerows to increase the size of fields. Alarm bells rang in some quarters, and an interest in the environment, and what we were doing to it, gradually started to emerge. Now there is a global awareness of the importance of bio-diversity, and efforts are being made, both nationally and internationally, to try to protect all native fauna and flora.

MONOCULTURE VERSUS BIODIVERSITY

Monoculture is the growing of a single plant in one area, like a field of wheat or an orchard of apple trees, which makes for easier management but has the potential to lead to shortages of individual soil nutrients or to the build-up of pests and diseases that are specific to the plant grown.

LEFT *Regimented rows of lettuces and cabbages, which are protected from birds by netting and from pests and diseases by chemicals, typify modern growing methods. In a wildlife garden, we are seeking to achieve the opposite effect.*

Most modern farming practices are monocultural, with the result that constant spraying with chemicals is needed to keep the crops free of pests, diseases and weeds. It is this arguably excessive use of sprays that has resulted in the loss of many native plants and animals throughout much of the world, not just in the West. Like farming, gardening can also be monocultural. Rose beds, closely mown lawns and plots of cabbages are all monocultural and depend on chemical controls to produce an unblemished result.

At the opposite end of the scale is biodiversity, whereby farmers and gardeners aim for as wide a variety of plant and animal species as possible within any given area. In the past, much time was spent studying plants and animals in their native habitats, but, with the declining numbers of some wildlife species and the reduction of their habitats, ecologists are now looking to gardens as potential homes for some of these threatened plants and animals.

ABOVE *You don't have to grow vegetables in patches that are all of a single type. A mixture looks more natural and also helps to retain the balance of nutrients in the soil, which means it is much healthier for the environment.*

THE NEED FOR A BALANCED APPROACH

The aim for a gardener who is interested in attracting wildlife is probably somewhere between the extremes of the unkempt bramble patch and the perfectly maintained garden. Such a gardener may want to include an element of monoculture, perhaps a lawn or a rose bed or two, but will also encourage a wider range of birds, insects, animals and wild plants within the garden as a whole.

Getting this balance of elements right is important: you want to have a garden that has something for all the members of the household to enjoy, but you also want to create interesting habitats where a wide range of native plants and animals can thrive.

THE IMPORTANCE OF HABITATS

*B*efore you can welcome wildlife into your garden, you will need to understand the different types of natural habitat. There are dozens of different habitats and each is home to a specific range of plants and animals. Some habitats, for example heather moorland and coastal cliffs, will be impossible to recreate in the average garden, but others could be created in almost any garden.

The woodland edge is where two habitats — woodland and meadow – meet, and as a result it is itself one of the richest habitats. There is a background of tall trees with an underlayer of shrubs, but enough light penetrates through for the ground to be covered in a wide range of plants that enjoy semi-shade conditions. As you go deeper into the woodland, so the range of plant species in the shrub layer and ground cover is reduced. As you emerge from the woodland, the trees and shrubs decrease and you get a meadow habitat. A woodland-edge habitat is readily created in any garden where there are a few mature trees by adding a range of native or ornamental berrying shrubs and a ground cover of woodland plants (*see page 42*).

HEDGEROWS

Mixed hedgerows are one of the most important habitats because they frequently provide a link, or wildlife corridor, between woods and fields. Planted with a variety of flowering and berrying shrubs, they provide food for insects, birds and small mammals and a safe haven in their closely entwined branches and in the dense undergrowth of wild flowers at their base. They also provide a refuge for wild flowers where the farmer's combine harvester or the gardener's lawnmower cannot reach. A mixed hedgerow makes a natural boundary for a garden in the country, particularly where the adjoining property is a field or wood. Details for creating a mixed hedgerow in your garden are given on page 44.

MEADOWS

Meadows are not naturally occurring ecological features but were created by farmers as pasture for grazing stock. With their mixture of grasses and wild flowers, they are an important habitat for many insects and small mammals.

BELOW *A woodland garden may easily be created where mature trees exist. Plant a few native shrubs and some ground cover to simulate the different layers found in a natural wood.*

POINTS TO CONSIDER

Insect-attracting plants for ground cover in woodland-edge or hedgerow-bottom habitats include the following:

- *Ajuga reptans* (bugle) – butterflies
- *Digitalis purpurea* (foxglove) – bumblebees
- *Hyacinthoides non-scripta* (bluebell) – bees and butterflies
- *Lamium maculatum* (white deadnettle) – bees and bumblebees
- *Primula vulgaris* (primrose) – butterflies and birds
- *Silene dioica* (red campion) – butterflies and moths
- *Stachys officinalis* (betony) – bees and butterflies
- *Viola odorata* (sweet violet) – butterflies and birds

The range of wild flowers found in any meadow will vary with the soil type and fertility and also with the drainage, so a damp water meadow will have ragged robin and lady's smock among its grasses, whereas a dry chalkland pasture may include wild thyme, bird's-foot trefoil and several vetches. A wildflower meadow can be planted in any garden where there is space, but check your soil first and then follow the instructions on page 46.

WATER AND WETLANDS

These are actually two different habitats. The first is that created within water for aquatic life, such as water beetles and tadpoles, and also for some wonderful plants, like the white water lily and water hawthorn. The second, wetland, comprises the permanently wet soil often found on river banks and next to ponds and lakes. It is the ideal home for all moisture-loving plants. In the garden, we can plan the two together as a garden pond and associated bog garden, which can be planted with either all native plants or a mixture of these with some introduced ornamentals. Refer to page 48 for advice on creating such a mixed habitat.

THE FLOWER BORDER

The border is not strictly a native habitat but a garden creation that generates its own range of wildlife if planted correctly. In a shady site it is more like a woodland edge, whereas in a sunny area it comes into its own as a major attraction for bees and butterflies. The border can be planted with just wild flowers, as in the other habitats, but, since many ornamental plants are rich in insect-attracting nectar, a mixture of plants from all over the world is most successful. It can be just herbaceous plants, as in the traditional summer-flowering herbaceous border, or it can be a mixture of bulbs, herbaceous plants and shrubs, which will extend the flowering season to cover most of the year, thus providing nectar and pollen in early spring and autumn when it is most needed.

SECRET PLACES

These are not official or individual habitats but simply places in which animals already in the garden can build nests and hibernate. Most animals are naturally wary of humans and need somewhere to hide in safety away from prying eyes; the compost heap, a pile of logs, a heap of leaves or a bramble patch or clump of nettles are all perfect.

ABOVE *Incorporating a wildlife pool into your garden enables you to grow moisture-loving plants as well as encouraging insects, fish, frogs, toads and newts to share your space.*

HONOURED GUEST OR UNWELCOME PEST?

There are so many animals and birds that are native to most areas that it can sometimes be quite difficult to decide which ones we want to bring into our gardens. Are we going to invite just a few butterflies, bees, frogs or hedgehogs, or are we going to encourage all manner of wildlife, including potential pests such as pigeons and rabbits? Somehow a balance has to be achieved between welcome visitors and unwanted nuisances.

Potential animal guests range from deer to tiny shrews. The larger mammals may be a problem, but fencing the perimeter of the garden will keep most at bay while leaving access for smaller mammals like hedgehogs, dormice and voles. Rabbits are a potential pest; again, fencing is an effective control, particularly if the base of the netting is fixed firmly underground. Most gardeners are happy to have badgers, even if they dig up parts of the lawn.

Grey squirrels are loved and loathed in almost equal measure; it is impossible to keep them out, so protecting individual trees and features is the only answer. Other mammals include hares, otters, pine-martens, water voles, stoats and weasels, but these are rarely found in gardens. Rats are a common pest in towns, where they inhabit the sewers, and on farms.

Some species of bats are in danger of extinction because their sources of food and shelter are under threat from modern farming and forestry methods. Our gardens can be refuges for bats, with sheds or special bat boxes providing shelter and plenty of insects available for food.

REPTILES AND AMPHIBIANS

Reptiles have dry, scaly skins and primarily live on land, whereas amphibians have bare, moist skins and breed in water. Reptiles include snakes and lizards. The venomous adder, which is extremely timid, is usually found on open heathland and sand dunes. The harmless grass snake can be found swimming in garden pools and nesting in compost heaps. The slow worm is actually a legless lizard, whose main diet is slugs, while the common lizard feeds on insects and spiders. Amphibians include frogs, toads and newts, and are usually welcome.

BIRDS

Hundreds of different bird species may visit gardens if food, water and nesting sites are provided. Most are welcome, but pigeons can decimate vegetable crops, bullfinches will eat fruit blossom, and sparrows and starlings may attack crocuses. Netting vegetable crops and cordon apples and placing soft fruit in cages will solve most problems, as will placing cotton thread over bulbs.

LEFT *What could be nicer than to find a hedgehog curled up asleep in a clump of* Digitalis purpurea *(foxgloves)? Small mammals like to find secret places where they can hide.*

INSECTS

There are thousands of different types of insect, and often the difficulty is knowing which are helpful friends and which are potential enemies. A useful rule of thumb is 'fast is friendly', so the scuttling beetle is a friend and the slow-moving aphid is an enemy. There are lots of animals and birds that feast on insects, and a wildlife garden needs a

ABOVE *A well-planned garden that provides food for animals and birds throughout the year can be a real lifesaver in the winter months for birds such as this bullfinch.*

few aphids to bring in their welcome predators such as ladybirds. Other insects include bees, butterflies, moths and dragonflies, which are generally welcome, and flies and wasps, which can be a nuisance. Removing wasp nests is a sensible precaution, as is avoiding leaving waste in the garden, which attracts flies. Ants, beetles, grasshoppers and crickets are fascinating creatures, and all are worth encouraging into the garden.

INVERTEBRATES

Slugs and snails can be a real nuisance in the garden but they do provide food for several species of birds, frogs and slow worms. Earthworms are essential, because their activities help to maintain soil fertility. Luckily, they are exceedingly common, because they are also food for many birds. Centipedes, millipedes and woodlice are all found in our gardens; centipedes live on insects but the other two eat plant material, both living and dead.

PLANNING YOUR WILDLIFE GARDEN

*I*f *you want to have both an attractive garden and a wildlife refuge, you will need to do some careful planning before you start. Decisions have to be made as to which species are really welcome in your garden and which you would rather avoid, the types of habitat you will enjoy tending and the wild flowers you want to grow. Your plan should be for a lovely garden in which many plants and animals will feel at home.*

Before doing anything, try to find out which animals are already in residence in your garden and might be disturbed if you start making changes. In a large garden, this may well take a year as you wait to see which plants come up and whether they attract bees and butterflies. Hedges, shrubs and trees should be carefully checked for nesting sites, and a watching brief kept to see who uses them. Visitors to a well-stocked bird table will indicate which birds are in your area and might like to take up residence, and it will also attract squirrels if they are in the neighbourhood. Check, too, on nocturnal life, including moths and hedgehogs, slugs and snails. Ponds and streams can be checked for frog- and toadspawn and a net can be used to discover the range of aquatic life that is already present.

YOUR FAMILY'S NEEDS

In all the effort about finding about wildlife, do not forget that your garden is your family's outside room and needs to be designed as a place in which all the members of the household can relax and enjoy themselves. Make lists of what everyone wants, and consider which of the requirements might be met. Find out if anyone has any strong feelings about wildlife – if one family member loathes snakes, then it is best not to encourage them.

PREPARING A PLAN

Draw a plan of your garden either by using an existing plan or by measuring the garden with a tape and transferring the measurements onto paper using an appropriate scale. A scale of 1–2cm to represent 1m (or 1in for 1yd) fits most gardens onto a convenient-sized piece of paper. This will give you an idea of the amount of space there is for different features; then you can start allocating space for specific purposes, such as a terrace next to the house, a grass area or lawn beyond, and hedges along the boundaries.

LEFT *To encourage birds into the garden, use a squirrel-proof feeder like this one. The blue tits will be in their element, and squirrels will be able to find sufficient food elsewhere.*

SOIL, ASPECT AND DRAINAGE

Before any planting is undertaken, you need to find out which plants will be happy in your garden; this will depend on the type of soil, the amount of sun or shade and the underlying drainage. It is also useful to know the depth of topsoil: a deep, rich topsoil will be wonderful for growing vegetables but useless for a wildflower meadow. A shady, damp garden will be good for woodland edge or wetland habitats but not so useful for attracting bees and butterflies.

YOUR VISITORS' NEEDS

Like any good potential host, you need to find out all about what your intended guests enjoy in the way of sleeping arrangements, food and drink. Hedgehogs, for instance, need safe hibernating nests of grass and leaves, plenty of beetles and caterpillars to eat and accessible water. Discover all you can about the requirements of different species and see how they could be met by creating a variety of habitats within your garden space and then furnishing them with a few home comforts, perhaps a bird table for birds and bowls of bread and milk for hedgehogs.

MAINTENANCE

All gardens, even those that appear quite wild, will need some maintenance, even if it is just an annual hacking back of the undergrowth. Decide on who is going to do it, remembering that if someone enjoys mowing grass it can be considered a spare-time hobby, but if they detest mowing it is always a chore. Tips for controlling potentially invasive plants are given on page 38.

BELOW *A garden pond will be an attraction for a wide range of animals. Frogs and toads will lay their eggs in the water, and small animals such as hedgehogs will come to drink.*

A REALLY WILD GARDEN

This is a garden for wildlife fanatics: the whole garden is a refuge for wild plants and animals, with nothing in it that would not be found in the countryside. The plan is based on a mature oak tree and a partially fallen tree, which provides log seats and whose decaying trunk is used by birds and insects. There is a small natural stone terrace by the house and an area of grass, cut in late summer to allow daffodils to naturalize and wild flowers to seed. Mown grass paths allow access through, and around, the meadow to the rest of the garden.

A large shrubbery fills one corner, with shrubs selected for their flowers, for bees and butterflies, and their fruit, for birds. A group of trees fills another corner, which is underplanted with woodland flowers. The only artificial structure is the shed, but this has been helped to blend in with its surroundings by having an ivy planted nearby, which has taken possession of one side. Near the shed is a patch of nettles provided specifically as food for hungry caterpillars and a tangle of brambles that provides flowers, fruits and nesting sites. The bramble and nettles are prevented from running wild over the garden by having any stems cut back that intrude too far and might be a nuisance to the human users of this area.

LEFT *Instead of creating a new area for a really wild garden, you could 'neglect' a corner of the existing one. In time, plants and wildlife will take over and make the corner their own.*

STAR PLANTS
Eupatorium cannabinum (hemp agrimony)
Filipendula ulmaria (meadowsweet)
Iris pseudacorus (yellow water iris)
Rubus fruticosus (bramble)
Salix alba (white willow)
Sorbus aria (whitebeam) and *S. aucuparia* (rowan)
Urtica dioica (stinging nettle)

In a low-lying corner is a small pond for frogs, toads and newts, with an extended bog garden nearby for wetland plants including meadowsweet, purple loosestrife, yellow water iris and hemp agrimony. The pond has a backdrop of hazel and willow to provide early pollen for bumblebees and sloping sides to allow birds and animals easy access to the water for drinking.

There is no bird table but extra food can be put out for birds in the winter, including hanging bunches of millet from tree branches and placing windfall apples on the ground. Fallen leaves from the shrubs and trees are heaped in piles for hedgehog and fieldmice nesting sites, and there is a small pile of stones near the pond for frogs and toads to hide among; shady spots are very welcome on hot days.

Is it a dream or could it become reality? It is perfectly possible and relatively simple to create and to maintain such a garden, but the owners may well feel that they themselves are the visitors and that the concerns of the resident wildlife are more catered for than their own. A balance is obviously needed to keep all parties happy.

Quercus robur *(oak) lends a feeling of maturity to the garden while playing host to many types of insect.*

Sorbus aria *(whitebeam) produces clusters of red berries in autumn that are loved by many birds.*

Salix alba *(white willow) produces delightful catkins in spring, and is a favourite of both insects and birds.*

Create a shrubbery *from a mixture of native plants to attract birds and butterflies.*

For ease of access *to all parts of the garden, leave a mown grass path through the meadow areas.*

This is the *larger of two wildflower areas within the garden.*

A pond *and adjacent bog garden will add considerably to the number of wildlife species attracted to the garden.*

RIGHT *This wild garden includes many of the usual garden features, but also incorporates two areas of wildflower meadow, a bog garden and a patch of nettles and brambles.*

A SUBURBAN RETREAT

A *family garden on the outskirts of a city or town can be the perfect place for parents and children to enjoy their outside space while watching any wild visitors. Most of the plants are selected for wildlife value, but ornamentals are included with the natives in order to provide plenty of colour in the beds and borders in summer. High on the agenda is the use of the garden as a refuge for town birds, so a well-stocked bird table is included as well as shrubs chosen for fruit and clumps of teasels and milk thistles for seeds.*

An attractive garden pond is sited in one corner, complete with adjacent pond garden and a sloping beach for easy access for visitors. A small paved area is positioned at one side of the pond so that the family can observe tadpoles and other aquatic life without getting their feet wet. A group of berrying shrubs close to the pond gives cover to small mammals visiting the water's edge, and there are several large rocks close to the pond that provide daytime resting places for toads.

A vegetable garden is included with a surrounding fence to keep out rabbits and other unwanted animals. On the inside of the fence are cordon fruit trees, which are easy to net from the birds in summer. By the vegetable

STAR PLANTS
🐾 *Amelanchier lamarckii* (snowy mespilus)
🐾 *Buddleja davidii* (butterfly bush) and *B. globosa*
🐾 *Dipsacus fullonum* (teasel)
🐾 *Malus sylvestris* (crab apple)
🐾 *Prunus padus* (bird cherry)
🐾 *Rubus fruticosus* (bramble)
🐾 *Silybum marianum* (milk thistle)

garden is an area for fallen leaves, compost heaps and a log pile, all of which can be used as nesting sites as well as providing a valuable resource for the garden. Further nesting sites will be provided in the future by several newly planted trees, but since these are not yet large enough some bird boxes have been erected.

With a growing family, there needs to be a paved terrace for outside meals and a mown lawn for games, but there is also an area of longer grass with spring bulbs and summer wild flowers. A bed for cornfield annuals is included as part of the children's garden, where they will grow *Helianthus annuus* (sunflowers), *Tagetes* (marigolds) and *Iberis amara* (candytuft). Beside the terrace, and in view of the house, are beds planted with flowers, which provide nectar for bees and butterflies.

There is an attractive herb garden to provide herbs for cooking and also to attract bees and butterflies. Simple wooden seats are placed both in the herb garden and elsewhere, so that the activities of the various garden inhabitants can be observed in comfort.

LEFT *Bring a touch of the wild into the suburbs by growing a mixture of annual summer* flowers such as Digitalis purpurea *(foxgloves) and a selection of poppies* (Papaver).

Birds will take some of the cordon fruit and blackberries – but there should be enough to please everybody.

The shed and compost area should provide a number of secret places ideal for hiding, nesting and hibernating.

The pond will be a haven for frogs and toads and a source of water for thirsty animals.

This area is the children's garden – in the centre is a bed of colourful cornfield annuals that they can easily grow from seed.

Malus sylvestris (crab apple) provides flowers and fruits for insects, birds and mammals.

The bee and butterfly garden includes Buddleja davidii (butterfly bush) in the corner, as well as other plants attractive to these insects.

The herb garden is formal in design, but includes plants that attract insects.

RIGHT This garden combines some of the practical requirements of a family, such as a lawn and terrace, with wilder areas that encourage animals, insects and birds to visit.

23

AN URBAN OASIS

T he owners of this small town garden are keen on conserving wildlife but realize that there is a real limitation on the range of species they can attract, both in terms of space within the garden and in the possible lack of natural habitats in the urban area around the garden. They have included plants rich in nectar for attracting bees and butterflies but have not got room for a wildflower meadow or many plants for caterpillars. A pond was considered overambitious, so a more modest water feature has been included instead.

In a small garden, great care is needed in the selection of each plant so that all contribute to the store of food for wildlife. A mixed hedge is not possible because there is inadequate room and no possibility of linking it to other hedges as a wildlife corridor. Instead, several berrying wall shrubs are included like pyracantha and cotoneaster, which provide food for birds and also safe nesting sites in the dense tangle of branches against the wall. Climbers are also a useful resource, and ivy is included on the garden wall, where its flowers, foliage, fruit and branches will be of maximum benefit to birds, bees, butterflies, other insects and small mammals. An eye should be kept on it to ensure that it does no damage to the wall. Other climbers are *Clematis montana* and *Lonicera periclymenum* (honeysuckle).

There really is not enough room for a wildlife pond, but a small ornamental raised pool with dripping jet provides interest for the owners and a source of water for visiting birds, including the local gang of house martins, who will use the water to make mud for their hanging nests. The water may even house a little frogspawn in the spring if any frogs wander into the garden from the surrounding urban jungle or a neighbouring garden.

The lawn has been replaced by a more usable paved area, where there is a bird table with ample room for hanging nets of nuts, balls of fat and space for chopped

ABOVE *In a small town garden, vegetables and herbs can be grown together to create a* *delightful mixture of shapes, colours, textures and scents. Wildlife will love it too.*

fruit and damp breadcrumbs on the top. There are several pots on the paving, one containing a cut-leaved elder; this has flowers and fruit like the species *Sambucus nigra* but the foliage is more decorative. Several pots will be planted seasonally with bulbs and *Erisymum cheiri* (wallflowers) in spring, and summer-flowering annuals including lobelia and *Tagetes patula* (French marigolds). One pot is left for cornfield annuals to be sown annually.

There are some animals who will not be very welcome: rats, a common inhabitant of towns, must be ruthlessly eradicated, and urban foxes can become a nuisance if there is a family in the vicinity.

STAR PLANTS

- *Cotoneaster horizontalis* (herringbone cotoneaster)
- *Hedera helix* (ivy)
- *Lobelia erinus*
- *Myosotis arvensis* (forget-me-not)
- *Pyracantha* 'Orange Glow' (firethorn)
- *Rosmarinus officinalis* (rosemary)

There is no room for a wildflower meadow or a lawn here, so paving, with plants in pots, is the best option.

Crataegus monogyna (hawthorn) has fragrant white spring blossom followed by red fruits that are eaten by birds and mice

Hedera helix (ivy) is an excellent evergreen climber for a boundary wall, and host to a range of creatures, but remember it is poisonous.

Buxus sempervirens (box) can be clipped to shape in the herb garden or left to grow more naturally.

Rosmarinus officinalis (rosemary) is an aromatic herb that is very attractive to bees.

Include an area for sitting or eating, so that you can enjoy the wildlife at first hand.

Include a water feature if you can – even a tiny, formal one will bring new and different species to the garden.

RIGHT *In a confined, paved town garden, wild areas have to be kept small and well under control. Use containers to increase the number of plants you can grow.*

CREATING YOUR GARDEN

2

Once you have finished planning your wildlife garden, it is time to start on practical tasks, such as choosing plants to attract specific creatures, buying and planting native plants and creating special habitats. All the techniques you will need in order to simulate a woodland edge, a hedgerow, a wildflower meadow or a wetland are explained here, as well as how to adapt existing garden beds and borders to maximize the numbers of insects, birds and animals visiting them.

LEFT *A mixture of* Chrysanthemum segetum *(corn marigolds),* Centaurea cyanus *(cornflowers) and* Papaver rhoeas *(corn poppies) is a delight.*

BIRDS • CHOICES

❶

OMNIVORES

Omnivorous birds feed on a wide range of different foods, which means that there is usually plenty for them to eat whatever the time of year. They include: the blue tit, which eats insects, seeds and nectar; the house sparrow, which likes seeds, buds and insects; the chaffinch, which eats seeds, weeds, caterpillars and even spiders; the blackbird, which eats insects, fruit and earthworms; and the robin, which likes insects, fruit, worms and snails. Other members of this group are the jay, which has a varied diet that can include small mammals; the somewhat less popular jackdaw, which raids other birds' nests for their eggs; and finally the magpie, which eats almost anything, including seeds, fruit, snails, slugs, spiders and carrion.

CHOICE CHECKLIST

❧ *Crataegus monogyna* (hawthorn) provides buds, nectar, fruit and insects.
❧ *Hedera helix* (ivy) provides nectar, fruit and shelter, and food for several caterpillars.

❧ *Rubus fruticosus* (bramble) provides buds, nectar, fruit and lots of insects and spiders plus ground-cover protection for nesting birds.

❷

INSECT-FEEDERS

Many birds, like the familiar swallow, are insect-feeders, deriving all or most of their food either from catching insects on the wing (in the case of swifts, swallows, house martins and flycatchers), by digging into the soil (green woodpeckers), or by collecting insects from the plants on which they are feeding (wrens, goldcrests and chiffchaffs). The more insect-attracting plants you grow in your garden the more insect-feeding birds will appear. The garden pond also provides mosquitoes and midges for swifts and swallows. A wildflower meadow is another insect-rich source for many birds, including wagtails. Most of these birds rarely visit bird tables, although in winter a few will take fallen seeds and crumbs.

CHOICE CHECKLIST

❧ *Achillea millefolium* (yarrow)
❧ *Angelica archangelica* (angelica)
❧ *Lavandula angustifolia* (lavender)

❧ *Lunaria annua* (honesty)
❧ *Melissa officinalis* (lemon balm)
❧ *Prunus padus* (bird cherry)
❧ *Solidago virgaurea* (golden rod)

3

SEED-EATERS

The goldfinch is an attractive small bird with a red face and yellow bars on its wings; teasels and thistles will readily attract it to the garden, as will dandelions left in the lawn to go to seed. Like the tree sparrow, brambling, greenfinch and crossbill, its diet consists entirely of seeds, whereas several other garden birds, like the siskin, linnet, dunnock, redpoll, nuthatch, great tit and reed bunting, relish seeds but also include insects in their diet, so that they do not go hungry when seeds are less available in spring and early summer. Another frequently seen garden bird, the bullfinch, likes seeds and insects but its real love is fruit buds, which makes it more of a pest than a welcome visitor. Most of these birds will visit bird tables in the winter for seeds and grain.

CHOICE CHECKLIST	
❧ *Dipsacus fullonum* (teasel)	❧ *Panicum miliaceum* (millet)
❧ *Helianthus annuus* (sunflower)	❧ *Silybum marianum* (milk thistle)
❧ *Onopordum acanthium* (cotton thistle)	❧ *Taraxacum officinale* (dandelion)

4

FRUIT-EATERS

Fruit-eating birds are easy to attract into your garden either by leaving windfall apples and other fruit on the ground in winter or by planting a range of plants that produce berries, like rowan trees and fruiting viburnums. Fruit-eating birds include the redwing and garden warbler, which eat only fruit, and fieldfares, mistle thrushes and blackcaps, which have fruit as a major part of their diet but may also eat seeds or insects. Several of the omnivorous birds, including blackbirds, robins, collared doves and pheasants, will happily eat fruit when it is available but eat a range of other food when the fruit season is over. Birds are attracted by the colour red, so red and red-orange berries are always eaten first, with white or yellow ones being left until late in winter.

CHOICE CHECKLIST	
❧ *Cotoneaster horizontalis* (herringbone cotoneaster)	❧ *Lonicera periclymenum* (honeysuckle)
❧ *Euonymus europaeus* (spindle)	❧ *Sambucus nigra* (elder)
❧ *Ilex aquifolium* (holly)	❧ *Sorbus aucuparia* (rowan)
	❧ *Viburnum opulus* (guelder rose)

BEES AND OTHER INSECTS • CHOICES

❶

BUMBLEBEES

There are several different species of bumblebee, which have thicker, hairier bodies than honeybees. They forage for food, pollinate flowers and sting predators like the honeybees and live in colonies with workers, drones and a queen bee. However, the colonies are much smaller and the bees do not survive the winter, leaving just the young queens hibernating underground to form new colonies in the spring. The largest is the buff-tailed bumblebee, with a yellow-and-black body and a buff-coloured tail. Other frequent visitors are the garden bumblebees, with white tails, the large red-tailed bumblebee (black body and red tail), the meadow bumblebee (red tail but yellow-and-black stripes) and the common carder bee (buff all over).

CHOICE CHECKLIST	
❧ *Antirrhinum majus* (snapdragon)	❧ *Lonicera periclymenum* (honeysuckle)
❧ *Digitalis purpurea* (foxglove)	❧ *Papaver rhoeas* (corn poppy)
❧ *Lamium maculatum* (white deadnettle)	❧ *Trifolium pratense* (red clover)

❷

HONEYBEES

Honeybees live in organized colonies or hives. A single fertile queen bee lives in the hive and lays eggs, which are then fed and guarded by thousands of sterile females, called worker bees, and a few hundred male drones. The nest is filled with an intricate honeycomb made from tree resin and water, and the spaces are filled with eggs, pollen or honey, made from flower nectar. The eggs develop into larvae, which are fed on pollen and honey until they emerge as bees. At the end of the summer, honey is stored for winter food during hibernation. Some colonies of wild bees live in hollow trees or cavity walls, and hives of honeybees are kept by farmers for the production of honey. Honeybees are major pollinators of wild flowers and fruit trees.

CHOICE CHECKLIST	
❧ *Calluna vulgaris* (ling)	❧ *Satureja montana* (winter savory)
❧ *Malus domestica* (apple)	❧ *Thymus vulgaris* (thyme)
❧ *Prunus domestica* (plum)	❧ *Tilia cordata* (lime)
❧ *Rosmarinus officinalis* (rosemary)	❧ *Trifolium repens* (white clover)

3

HOVERFLIES

There are nearly 250 different kinds of hoverfly, which get their name from their habit of hovering over plants before landing to take nectar and pollen. Most of the species are mimics and take on the colouring of wasps, honey- or bumblebees to provide a defence from predators. However, they are all completely harmless, having no sting, and use their protective colouring and darting speed to keep out of danger. They are very useful insects to attract into the garden because their slug-like larvae feed on aphids, some managing to consume up to 800 aphids in a two-week larval period. They are also useful pollinators. Hoverflies have short tongues and favour flowers with exposed pollen and nectar, such as plants of the carrot and daisy families.

CHOICE CHECKLIST

❧ *Calendula officinalis* (marigold)
❧ *Clematis vitalba* (old man's beard)
❧ *Foeniculum vulgare* (fennel)

❧ *Hedera helix* (ivy)
❧ *Levisticum officinale* (lovage)
❧ *Tagetes patula* (French marigold)

4

LADYBIRDS

There are many different types of ladybird, of which some are red with black spots, others are yellow with black spots, and yet others black with yellow spots. The numbers of spots vary but the most common are the seven-spot ladybird and the smaller two-spot ladybird. Their bright colour warns predators that they are poisonous and should be left alone. They are a friend to gardeners because all ladybirds are voracious aphid-eaters, as are their slate-blue, rather ugly, larvae. Ladybirds lay their eggs on aphid-infested plants so that when the larvae emerge there is ample food for them. The adults hibernate in cold weather and search out cracks in woodwork in which to spend the winter. Hundreds will huddle together awaiting spring.

CHOICE CHECKLIST

❧ *Rosa* species (roses) are host to several aphids and, consequently, ladybirds.
❧ *Trifolium pratense* (red clover); the 24-spot ladybird feeds on plants like clover.

❧ *Urtica dioica* (stinging nettle) has lots of resident aphids, and ladybirds are frequent visitors.

BUTTERFLIES · CHOICES

❶

ARISTOCRAT BUTTERFLIES

Early entomologists gave the name of 'aristocrats' to the largest and most colourful butterflies in the countryside and then gave them aristocratic names like purple emperor, red admiral and painted lady. Most of them hibernate as adults during the winter, although the red admiral, painted lady and Camberwell beauty may not survive cold winters. The small tortoiseshell is the most often seen, followed by the red admiral and the peacock. The red admiral, small tortoiseshell, peacock and comma all lay their eggs on stinging nettles, which are the caterpillars' food plant. The larvae of the white admiral feed on honeysuckle and their low numbers are now increasing, whereas the purple emperor, which feeds on sallow trees, is now rarely seen.

CHOICE CHECKLIST

- *Aster novi-belgii* (Michaelmas daisy)
- *Buddleja davidii* (butterfly bush)
- *Centranthus ruber* (red valerian)
- *Hebe salicifolia* (shrubby veronica)
- *Origanum vulgare* (marjoram)
- *Sedum spectabile* (ice plant)

❷

BLUES, COPPERS AND HAIRSTREAKS

These are all small butterflies and mostly swift flyers; the blues and coppers have bright-coloured wings, whereas the hairstreaks are more muted, usually with a white-line 'hairstreak' on the underside of the wings.

The blues and coppers are found in grassland, where bird's-foot trefoil, kidney vetch and dock provide them with food for their caterpillars, and the hairstreaks in woodlands and glades, where their caterpillars feed on blackthorn, oaks and elms. The adult butterflies of the common and holly blue and the small copper are often seen in gardens seeking nectar. Creating a wildflower meadow with clovers and vetches will encourage these butterflies. The white-letter hairstreak will visit brambles and privet.

CHOICE CHECKLIST

- *Hedera helix* (ivy)
- *Lavandula angustifolia* (lavender)
- *Mentha spicata* (spearmint)
- *Origanum vulgare* (marjoram)
- *Rubus fruticosus* (bramble)
- *Thymus vulgaris* (thyme)

❸

WHITE AND YELLOW BUTTERFLIES

These butterflies are predominantly white or yellow and most of their caterpillar food plants are in the cabbage and pea families – the Brassicaceae and Papilionaceae. An exception is the brimstone, whose caterpillars will feed only on buckthorn and whose bright yellow wings may have given the name *butter*fly to this group of insects. The brimstone hibernates as a butterfly, whereas the others mostly overwinter as chrysalises. Most of the group have black markings on their wings, which act as a warning to predators that the wings are poisonous. The clouded yellow, brimstone and orange-tip butterflies are all welcome visitors, but perhaps not the large and small white butterflies, the cabbage whites, whose caterpillars devour cabbage leaves.

CHOICE CHECKLIST

- *Aubrieta deltoidea*
- *Centranthus ruber* (red valerian)
- *Erysimum cheiri* (wallflower)
- *Hesperis matronalis* (sweet rocket)
- *Lunaria annua* (honesty)
- *Myosotis arvensis* (forget-me-not)

❹

BROWN AND FRITILLARY BUTTERFLIES

The brown butterflies all have false 'eyes' on either the upper or lower surface of the wings, which are intended to confuse predators. All but the marbled white are brown in colour with occasional orange markings. They spend the winter as caterpillars eating grass; the adults emerge during the summer and are mostly to be found in grassland and pasture. The gatekeeper and meadow brown are regular garden visitors for nectar, and creating a wildflower meadow may encourage other browns.

The fritillaries inhabit woodland glades; they have orange or brown wings with speckled markings. The caterpillars of several fritillaries depend on violets for their food plant, and a number of the fritillaries are in serious decline.

CHOICE CHECKLIST

- *Hebe salicifolia* (shrubby veronica)
- *Iberis amara* (candytuft)
- *Lavandula angustifolia* (lavender)
- *Ligustrum vulgare* (privet)
- *Origanum vulgare* (marjoram)
- *Thymus vulgaris* (thyme)

POND LIFE • CHOICES

❶

FROGS

Frogs, toads and newts are all amphibians and need water for breeding and for part of their life cycle. Eggs are laid in the water, and the first stage of life, the tadpole, swims in the water before developing into an adult, which comes out onto dry land. Frogs are frequent visitors to garden ponds because their natural habitats, field ponds, have become filled in or polluted. During the summer they will travel considerable distances in search of water. Frogs have a smooth skin and long legs with bold markings. They are useful garden inhabitants because the tadpoles feed on algae and the adult frogs eat insects, slugs and snails. The usual garden frog is the common frog, but other species, such as the marsh frog and the edible frog, also occur.

CHOICE CHECKLIST

❧ *Butomus umbellatus* (flowering rush); this marginal plant gives cover to frogs when they breed in the pond

❧ *Nymphaea alba* (white water lily); the leaves are used by adult frogs for basking and also to give cover to protect tadpoles from predators.

❷

TOADS

Like frogs, toads hibernate in winter, finding a damp spot under stones or logs not far from their breeding ponds. In the early spring, the toads awaken and migrate back to the pond, often in large numbers, and often climbing walls and crossing busy roads on the way, during which many are killed by traffic. Toadspawn is produced in long double strings of eggs, which are often wrapped around water plants. The tadpoles live in the pond before emerging as adult toads to live on dry land. Toads tend to be solitary and live under logs or vegetation during the day, emerging at evening to feed on insects and small animals. The usual toad found in or near garden ponds is the common toad; a slightly smaller and faster one is the natterjack.

CHOICE CHECKLIST

❧ *Iris pseudacorus* (yellow water iris); marginal plants planted on the edge of the pond help protect small toads from predators as they leave the water for dry land.

❧ *Mentha aquatica* (water mint); toads twine strands of eggs around the underwater stems.

❸

NEWTS

Newts are not often seen out of water (they spend most of their time in the pond and even hibernate in the mud at the bottom) but they will emerge to hibernate under rockery stones if these are placed near the pond. The smooth newt is the most common species and is found in most areas; the smaller palmate newt is found in moorlands and heaths; and the great crested newt spends most of its time in the water. The latter is now very rare and protected by law. Newts lay their eggs singly, attached to a submerged leaf, which is wrapped around the egg for protection. The tadpoles have external gills and the tadpole stage is longer than in frogs or toads. Newts emerge in the evening to feed on insects and slugs.

CHOICE CHECKLIST

❧ Newts will colonize any small body of water where there are underwater oxygenating plants, aquatic plants like water lilies and marginal plants like

Butomus umbellatus, *Iris pseudacorus*, *Mentha aquatica* and *Menyanthes trifoliata*, which provide leaves for egg-laying and cover for tadpoles.

❹

DRAGONFLIES

Another inhabitant of garden ponds is the dragonfly, which lays its eggs just below the surface of the water. The eggs hatch out as larvae, known as nymphs; these may spend two to five years in the pond before climbing out up the leaves or stem of a water plant to shed their skin and emerge as dragonflies. The adults feed on midges by swooping over the water to catch them in flight. The largest dragonfly is the emperor, with a wingspan of 10cm (4in) and a bright blue abdomen in the male and green in the female. Other dragonflies are separated into hawkers, which have long wings and thin bodies and restlessly patrol their territory, and darters, which have thicker bodies and spend much of their time clinging to waterside vegetation.

CHOICE CHECKLIST

❧ *Iris pseudacorus* (yellow water iris); the leaves are used by the nymph to climb up out of the water to moult and the dragonfly to emerge.

❧ *Lythrum salicaria* (purple loosestrife); used as a perch while devouring insects.
❧ *Nymphaea alba* (white water lily); used as resting places by dragonflies.

BUYING NATIVE PLANTS

When the first wildlife gardens were suggested in the 1970s, it was extremely difficult to buy plants or even seeds of wild flowers. As the whole subject of wildlife and conservation has grown, however, so the nurseries have followed, and it is now much easier to obtain both plants and seeds of many native plants. Some wild flowers have become so popular that garden centres carry a range of wildflower seeds, including ready-made mixtures.

If you are really interested in conserving native plants then it is important to check the provenance of the seed you buy, that is, the place from which it originates. Some of the commercial seed available may have been collected in another country and is, therefore, not a true native of your area. It may even show some differences, possibly having brighter flowers or larger leaves. Look for local seed and

try to buy only from one of the nurseries specializing in wild flowers who are usually meticulous as to where their seeds are collected.

It is possible to collect seed from plants growing in the wild but this must be done sparingly and only of common species that are not on the endangered plant list. Ask permission from the landowner first and take only enough

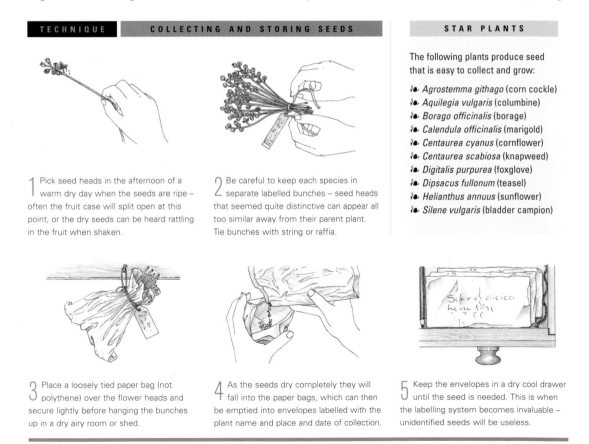

| TECHNIQUE | COLLECTING AND STORING SEEDS | STAR PLANTS |

STAR PLANTS

The following plants produce seed that is easy to collect and grow:

- *Agrostemma githago* (corn cockle)
- *Aquilegia vulgaris* (columbine)
- *Borago officinalis* (borage)
- *Calendula officinalis* (marigold)
- *Centaurea cyanus* (cornflower)
- *Centaurea scabiosa* (knapweed)
- *Digitalis purpurea* (foxglove)
- *Dipsacus fullonum* (teasel)
- *Helianthus annuus* (sunflower)
- *Silene vulgaris* (bladder campion)

1 Pick seed heads in the afternoon of a warm dry day when the seeds are ripe – often the fruit case will split open at this point, or the dry seeds can be heard rattling in the fruit when shaken.

2 Be careful to keep each species in separate labelled bunches – seed heads that seemed quite distinctive can appear all too similar away from their parent plant. Tie bunches with string or raffia.

3 Place a loosely tied paper bag (not polythene) over the flower heads and secure lightly before hanging the bunches up in a dry airy room or shed.

4 As the seeds dry completely they will fall into the paper bags, which can then be emptied into envelopes labelled with the plant name and place and date of collection.

5 Keep the envelopes in a dry cool drawer until the seed is needed. This is when the labelling system becomes invaluable – unidentified seeds will be useless.

HINTS AND TIPS

🍃 Never take fully grown plants or collect seeds from the wild unless you know what you are doing is legal and you have the land-owner's permission to do it.

🍃 Seek advice from specialist nurseries or garden centres regarding the best way to obtain the plants you wish to grow.

🍃 Be careful not to plant species that will take over not only your own garden but also your neighbours' (*see page 39*).

🍃 When plants are established, collect your own seeds.

seed for your own use. Once you have started growing wild flowers it should be possible and much easier to harvest your own seed each year for future use.

COLLECTING NATIVE PLANTS FROM THE WILD

It is against the law to dig up plants in the wild without first asking permission of the owner of the land. There is also a list of protected species that it is illegal to pick, dig up, damage or sell. There are also certain areas of high nature conservation interest, including nature reserves, and areas of special scientific interest in which all plants are protected by law. If you cannot find a plant in a nursery and know that there is a plentiful supply locally, then seek the advice of your local nature conservation trust or botanical society and the land-owner's permission. It is more prudent to start plants from seed or to purchase plants from a specialist nursery.

BUYING NATIVE PLANTS

Many native plants are available from specialist nurseries and some can be bought from garden centres. The nurseries may supply a range of size of plants, depending on the species and type of plant.

Many herbaceous perennials are available as trays of 'plugs' – small rooted plants ready to be planted out in a wildflower meadow or woodland garden. These are relatively inexpensive and very useful when establishing large numbers of individual species. Where only a few plants are needed, perhaps for a clump in the flower border, then small pots of plants may be a simpler and better alternative.

Hedging plants are usually planted as bare-root seedlings or transplants. Seedlings are a single rooted stem 30–60cm

(12–24in) high, whereas transplants have stronger root systems and the stem or stems are 45–90cm (18–36in) high. Larger plants can be used but the transplants have the highest success rate and are relatively inexpensive.

Many native shrubs are used in hedging, and it is possible to buy hedging-sized plants for general planting. However, where plants are to be planted individually larger plants may be better. Shrubs that are sold in containers have compost around their root balls and are often much easier to establish than bare-root plants.

Native trees are usually grown from seed and are available as seedlings and transplants. Most trees, particularly oak and beech, thrive most successfully if planted as small specimens of about 1.8m (6ft) high.

ABOVE *Most native wild flowers can be obtained in seed form from specialist nurseries. Once established in your garden, many will self-seed to provide new plants for following years.*

PLANTING AND GROWING NATIVE PLANTS

*P*lanting native plants in a wildlife garden can be a simple affair or it can be a little more ambitious, such as sowing a cornfield (see opposite), planting a woodland (see page 42), planting a hedgerow (see page 44) or creating a wildflower meadow (see page 46). Maintenance will be different, because no longer can you reach for the spray gun when a pest or some weeds appear. Native plants are adapted to local soil and climate and tend to be more vigorous than garden plants, so strict control may be needed to prevent them taking over.

Many native plants come up from seed each year in the spring, produce leaves and flowers, set seed and then die as the cold weather arrives. These include cornfield annuals, which used to grow between the rows of corn in the farmers' fields. They were adapted to the annual routine of ploughing, sowing and harvesting – the seeds germinated with the corn, produced flowers and set seed, which was then shed as the corn was harvested. The shed seeds were turned into the soil as the farmer ploughed. Many such plants have suffered from the use of weedkillers applied to ensure that the harvested corn is uncontaminated. They are now available to gardeners, however, who can have their own colourful mini cornfield year after year.

STAR PLANTS

The following are the most colourful cornfield annuals:

- *Agrostemma githago* (corn cockle)
- *Centaurea cyanus* (cornflower)
- *Chrysanthemum segetum* (corn marigold)
- *Papaver rhoeas* (corn poppy)

INVASIVE PLANTS

Some native plants are very vigorous and will need to be kept under control if they are not to take over and turn the garden into a glorified nettle and bramble patch. For this reason, a few plants are considered too great a potential problem and have been excluded from the plant directory at the end of this book. They include most of the thistles, which, although extremely popular with seed-eating birds and vital for providing food for the caterpillars of the painted lady butterfly, have a tendency to spread their large numbers of seeds all over the garden and into neighbouring fields and gardens, which would make you extremely unpopular. The two thistles included in the directory – *Silybum marianum* (milk thistle) and *Onopordum acanthium* (cotton thistle) – are less generous with their seeds, and the relatively few seedlings are easily seen and removed should too many appear. Other plants that have been excluded are creeping buttercup and bindweed; this is not because they have no wildlife value, but because they are already major weeds in our gardens and it seems unwise to introduce more of them purposefully.

LEFT Centaurea cyanus (corn-flowers) produce striking, bright blue flowers that stand out vividly among the creams, reds and yellows of the other flowers in this border.

PROJECT **SOWING A WILDFLOWER CORNFIELD**

1 Choose a sunny site and prepare a seed bed by forking over the ground to remove all the weeds, then treading the ground to firm it before raking the topsoil level.

2 Create your own seed mixture or buy a ready-made mix of cornfield annuals. If you want to include some corn for an authentic cornfield look, then look for a seed mixture that includes wheat, barley or oats.

3 In early spring, rake the topsoil thoroughly in order to produce a fine tilth, just before sowing. Then apply a general-purpose fertilizer.

4 Mix the seeds with fine sand and then scatter them thinly over the prepared area. The sand will make even distribution easier and show where you have already sown.

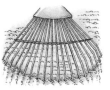

5 Rake the soil with a spring-tine rake so that the soil partially covers the seed, then water the seed with a watering can with a fine-rose head.

6 As the seedlings grow, it may be necessary to thin out plants growing too closely together; transplant the thinnings to any gaps in the cornfield.

7 The plants should flower in mid- to late summer. When the flowers have faded and seed heads formed, collect seed for use the following year.

8 To ensure a cornfield next year, fork over the bed in autumn or early spring. Remove any old plants in spring and prepare a seed bed, before repeating steps 4 to 7.

POSSIBLE PROBLEM PLANTS

Some native plants, such as yarrow, lesser celandine and toadflax, have strong creeping rootstocks or tubers; these can become a nuisance in an ornamental border but are excellent in a wildflower meadow. Dandelion, curled dock and plantain, all of which very readily set seed, also need to be confined to the wildflower meadow.

Brambles and stinging nettles, both indispensable for the wildlife garden, need to be confined to the remoter parts of the garden; you must ruthlessly eliminate any shoots that appear beyond the defined boundaries of their areas.

The key to controlling all these plants is to check every autumn whether they have started to spread too vigorously and to remove any trespassing plants.

PLANTS THAT NEED CONTROLLING

The following will all take over your garden unless you keep a very careful check on their spread:

- *Achillea millefolium* (yarrow)
- *Linaria vulgaris* (toadflax)
- *Onopordum acanthium* (cotton thistle)
- *Plantago major* (great plantain)
- *Ranunculus ficaria* (lesser celandine)
- *Rubus fruticosus* (bramble)
- *Rumex crispus* (curled dock)
- *Silybum marianum* (milk thistle)
- *Taraxacum officinale* (dandelion)
- *Urtica dioica* (stinging nettle)

CONTROLLING PESTS AND DISEASES

*O*nce you decide to encourage wildlife in your garden, you must stop using pesticides, fungicides and weedkillers. Pesticides kill the good insects as well as the pests; slug pellets kill hedgehogs; and fungicides and weedkillers affect earthworms. Initially this may lead to infestations of greenfly (aphids) on the roses, but once the ladybirds, hoverflies and lacewings have increased in numbers, they should keep the greenfly at an acceptable level.

A healthy, well-grown plant will tend to be unaffected by an infestation of greenfly or an attack of mildew, and will grow away quickly from any damage. Always grow plants that are suitable for the soil in your garden, and place them so that they get the right amount of sunlight and moisture. Enrich your soil with as much organic matter as you can find, whether it is garden compost, leaf mould or spent mushroom compost, and add well-rotted farmyard manure in place of artificial fertilizers. An organically rich soil will feed the soil micro-organisms and increase their activity. It will also supply the plants with a balanced range of nutrients and encourage root growth.

PEST CONTROL WITHOUT CHEMICALS

The next stage is to encourage natural predators that feed on the pests. Ladybirds and their larvae, hoverfly larvae and lacewings and their larvae all eat massive amounts of aphids, so planting flowers whose nectar attracts these predators will bring these useful insects into the garden. Frogs, toads and magpies eat slugs, so a garden pond will provide a place for the frogs and toads and nearby tall trees a nest site for magpies. Hedgehogs also eat slugs, so providing places for hedgehogs to hide will help control slugs. (Note that, because the pellets we put down to kill slugs also kill hedgehogs, natural control of these pests is thwarted by our intervention.) Many birds eat insects and caterpillars, so creating a range of habitats for different

ABOVE *Companion planting can sometimes help to reduce the incidence of certain pests and diseases. The close proximity of alliums is thought to prevent blackspot occurring on roses.*

birds will be a help in keeping insects and other pests at an acceptable level. There will always be a few pests, or the predators would go hungry and might die out themselves; it is a question of achieving an acceptable balance. After all, a few holes in the lettuces is a small price to pay to ensure the safety of all the inhabitants of the garden.

Other methods of controlling pests include companion planting – planting two plants together, where one of the plants controls the pests or diseases of the other. Planting *Tagetes patula* (French marigolds) in the greenhouse can reduce whitefly infestations, and planting strong-smelling

---

HINTS AND TIPS

🍂 Do not lose heart in the early stages if pests seem to be thriving – it takes time to achieve the right balance.

🍂 Always destroy infected plant material, so that diseases cannot be transmitted to other plants via garden compost.

alliums next to roses may reduce blackspot. Similarly, planting flowers that attract aphid-eating larvae next to plants that are susceptible to greenfly should keep infestations down. Certainly, there is an advantage in mixed planting rather than having beds of a single plant like roses.

PHYSICAL CONTROLS

It is possible to control some pests, particularly caterpillars, by picking the grubs off the leaves and flowers when you find them. Likewise, slugs can be collected as they appear in the evening and dispatched in a jar of salt water, and the tips of plants covered in blackfly can be nipped off and destroyed. You can also put up barriers, like placing a fine mesh net over the cabbages to prevent the cabbage white butterfly getting in to lay her eggs, and using a finer mesh to keep out fleabeetles, carrot root fly and other flying pests.

GOOD HUSBANDRY

One way of helping to control diseases is to remove infected parts of the plant as soon as they are seen. The infected material should be burnt immediately or removed from the garden (probably to the municipal dump, although do not put it into the containers marked 'greenery for compost'). Similarly, do not put it on your compost heap because the heat generated as the material rots down is not always sufficient to kill the spores of the fungi causing the disease, and so you could simply spread the disease around the garden via your compost. Where plants have shown signs of disease, remove all the old stems and leaves as they die down in the autumn; do not leave them on the ground to overwinter. Although the use of fungicides is not possible for a wildlife garden, there are several safe organic methods available for the control of most diseases.

TECHNIQUE	CONTROLLING BLACKSPOT ON ROSES

1 Plant roses that are known to be resistant to blackspot, such as *Rosa rugosa*. Check the plants in spring before buds burst and remove any infected shoots.

2 Check the plants regularly in summer and remove any leaves with blackspot as soon as they appear.

3 In autumn, clear all fallen leaves from below the roses and burn or destroy all infected material. Mulch the soil with compost and manure.

4 Consider planting companion plants like alliums with the roses. This is said to reduce the occurrence of blackspot.

STAR PLANTS

When planting vegetables and fruit, use companion plants to control pests and diseases. Try planting some of these plants together:

- *Allium schoenoprasum* (chives) – with apples or carrots
- *Borago officinalis* (borage) – with tomatoes or in the orchard
- *Hyssopus officinalis* (hyssop) – with brassicas
- *Iberis amara* (candytuft) – with brassicas
- *Ocimum basilicum* (basil) – with tomatoes
- *Salvia officinalis* (sage) – with carrots or brassicas
- *Satureja montana* (winter savory) – with broad beans or onions
- *Tagetes patula* (French marigold) – with tomatoes
- *Tropaeolum majus* (nasturtium) – with apples, brassicas or cucumbers
- *Urtica dioica* (stinging nettle) – in the orchard

THE WOODLAND EDGE

*W*oodlands are a rich repository of wildlife because native trees harbour large numbers of insects, which in turn attract insect-eating birds. Bees visit the flowers for pollen and nectar, and birds and squirrels nest in the branches. Non-native trees are not nearly as rich in wildlife, with fewer insects having adapted to using them as host plants, but they still have a valuable role to play in providing nectar, fruit and nesting sites.

If you are lucky enough to have an area of existing woodland in your garden, then you are already on your way to establishing a species-rich woodland garden. Start by checking the actual trees in the woodland, noting their species, type and condition. If any trees are growing too close together, they may need thinning in order to provide them with sufficient room for growth and enough light for health. Diseased and dead trees may need to be cut down. Consider leaving one or two dead or dying trees, because they will provide food for many insects and invertebrates, which are then food for birds like woodpeckers, and any holes in the tree trunks will provide nesting sites for bees, mice, squirrels and birds. Add additional trees where there are gaps in the canopy, then consider whether there is room beneath for an under-layer of native shrubs and some ground-covering herbaceous plants. Planting three such layers within your woodland will provide an attractive setting that is true to nature, and one that, in its diversity, will be home to all manner of wildlife.

ABOVE *The dappled sunlight in a woodland garden produces ideal conditions for some* shade-loving plants such as the white-flowered *Anemone nemorosa (wood anemone).*

TECHNIQUE	PLANTING WOODLAND BULBS

1 Lift bulbs after flowering and before the leaves have died down (such plants are known as 'in the green').

2 Keep in damp compost or plant immediately where they are to flower. Avoid planting them when there is frost on the ground.

3 Dig a hole large and deep enough to allow the roots to be spread out below ground level. Firm the soil well over the roots. Water well if the ground is dry.

PROJECT   **PLANTING NEW WOODLAND WITH SMALL TREES**

1 Mark out the total area to be planted as woodland, and then either clear the ground by digging it over or closely mow the grass to an even height.

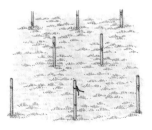

2 Place canes or markers in the proposed positions for trees and shrubs. Adjust the markers so that the lines are not too rigid. Your aim should be for a natural-looking woodland, not a tree plantation.

3 Dig holes and plant the trees. Check the soil to see if it needs improving with compost or leaf mould before covering up the tree roots. There are proprietary tree planting composts available if required.

4 To assist growth, place a tree mat around the roots to suppress weeds, and a 'tree tube' around the trunk to increase growth and protect the young plant from deer and rabbit damage.

5 Leave the tree tube in place until the trunk of the tree splits the tube. Regularly check the trees during the early years: the tubes may get blown over in a strong wind. You may need to water in dry periods.

STAR PLANTS

The following trees are host to the number of insect species indicated:

- *Quercus robur* (oak) – 300
- *Salix alba* (white willow) – 250
- *Betula pendula* (birch) – 230
- *Crataegus monogyna* (hawthorn) – 150
- *Populus nigra* (black poplar) – 100
- *Alnus glutinosa* (alder) – 90
- *Pinus sylvestris* (Scots pine) – 90
- *Malus sylvestris* (crab apple) – 90
- *Fagus sylvatica* (beech) – 60
- *Fraxinus excelsior* (ash) – 40

WOODLAND BULBS

Several bulbous plants, including *Galanthus nivalis* (snow-drops) and *Hyacinthoides non-scripta* (bluebells), are much easier to establish when planted 'in the green', i.e. after flowering, than as dry bulbs. Such plants are not always easy to get hold off, but you may find friends who have clumps to spare and they are also obtainable from specialist nurseries. Do not be tempted to dig up these bulbs in the wild because it is against the law. Bluebells, in particular, will multiply rapidly, and a few clumps will soon spread to produce an impressive blue carpet in spring.

NEW WOODLAND

It is possible to start a wood from scratch (*see above*). In the early years, grass will grow between the trees, but once a canopy has been established the ground beneath can be planted with bluebells and other woodland plants.

Local grants may be available, so check with your planning authority. Work out a plan for the woodland or tree belt: it is easier to use a grid system with trees and large shrubs planted at 3m (10ft) spacings. Space larger trees like oak, ash and beech 9m (30ft) apart and place faster-growing, smaller trees like hazel and hawthorn in between.

HEDGEROWS

The traditional mixed hedgerows that border many fields and lanes are a vital link in the chain that supports wildlife. The best wildlife hedges are those that are joined to other hedges or areas of woodland: this network of hedges and trees provides 'wildlife corridors' along which animals can safely travel from one area to another. Garden hedges may exist in isolation from this network, but they are still a valuable resource for wildlife.

Many garden hedges consist of a single species, like beech, hornbeam, holly, privet or yew. These hedges are a good choice where the garden is fairly formal, because they can be regularly cut to form a neat and tidy barrier, but they are not particularly wildlife-friendly. Although the dense branches may provide cover for small mammals and nesting sites for birds, and many contain spiders and other insects, the frequent cutting of the hedge will mean that it produces little or nothing in the way of flowers or fruit.

Less formal hedges of *Rosa rugosa* or *Berberis* are often used to separate different areas of the garden, and these hedges are usually allowed to flower and fruit with just an occasional cut to keep the growth under control. The

flowers of both of the above hedging plants are visited by bees and bumblebees, the fruit and any resident insects are eaten by birds, and nesting sites may be found within the protection of their prickly branches.

MIXED NATIVE HEDGEROWS

Where the garden is informal and the boundaries abut fields or woods, it should be possible to plant a traditional hedge with a mixture of species. These hedges are never as tidy as a single-species hedge but are much more interesting, with a variety of leaf colours and textures and, if left uncut until late in the season, plenty of flowers and fruit to add to their appeal. Once the hedge is growing well, plants such as dog roses, honeysuckle, brambles and old man's beard can be planted to scramble through it, adding extra colour and interest. Plant a selection of low-growing wild flowers such as primroses, violets and red campion at the base of the hedge; these will give early-spring interest and add to the overall pleasure. When the hedge is fully established, it will require no more than a yearly trim. The coarser plants growing in and around it should be removed from the hedge base to keep it in order.

LEFT *The natural untidiness of a hedgerow is part of its attraction. Once established, scrambling plants will add their form and colour to the hedge, and wildlife will colonize it.*

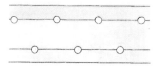

1 Hedges are planted in two rows usually 30cm (12in) apart. The plants, spaced at 45cm (18in) intervals, are staggered between the rows: a 10m (33ft) hedge needs 45 plants.

2 Plant in winter, using hedging plants; these are usually supplied bare-root in bundles of ten plants and need to be planted as soon as they arrive, or be kept damp.

3 Dig a trench 30cm (12in) deep and 60cm (24in) wide along the line of the hedge; check that there is no impeded drainage.

4 When ready to plant, soak any roots that have dried out in water before planting. Space the plants out along the trench using the ratio for your chosen mixture.

5 Backfill with the excavated soil mixed with compost or manure and water-retaining crystals. Firm the roots in well.

6 Water the trench after planting and mulch with a 7.5cm (3in) depth of bark or compost. Weed the plants and water in dry weather until established and growing well.

SELECTION OF SPECIES

Many farm hedgerows were originally single-species hedges of hawthorn that gradually became mixed as other plants drifted in with the wind or were carried by birds and small mammals. Nowadays we start by planting a mixed hedge, but usually still allow the hawthorn to predominate. There are various hedgerow mixtures, so select one with plants suitable for your soil. Most hedging plants are suitable for most soils, but chalky soils will favour a mixture with the following ratio: 5 hawthorn: 3 dogwood: 3 field maple: 2 spindle: 2 hazel: 1 wayfaring tree; whereas on a damp soil willow (*Salix*), guelder rose and dogwood will flourish.

STAR PLANTS

- *Acer campestre* (field maple)
- *Cornus sanguinea* (dogwood)
- *Corylus avellana* (hazel)
- *Crataegus monogyna* (hawthorn)
- *Euonymus europaeus* (spindle)
- *Prunus spinosa* (sloe)
- *Salix caprea* (goat willow)
- *Sambucus nigra* (elder)
- *Viburnum lanata* (wayfaring tree)
- *Viburnum opulus* (guelder rose)

WILDFLOWER MEADOWS

A grassy meadow can be full of life — lie down among the mixture of grasses and wild flowers and you can watch spiders building webs between blades of grass, caterpillars of the dingy skipper and common blue butterflies munching away on the leaves of bird's-foot trefoil, ants making tracks in the undergrowth and dancing bees collecting nectar from the white clover. Contrast this vibrant scene with the sterility of a closely mown, weed-free lawn.

Unfortunately, creating such a perfect wildflower meadow is not as easy as it sounds, because the average garden soil is high in nutrients and our native grasses grow extremely well, often defeating the attempts of other plants to survive. Yarrow, docks and plantains are among the few plants able to compete with grass. If the soil in your garden is deep and fertile, it may be necessary to remove some of the topsoil (keep it to add to flower beds and vegetable areas) and mix the remaining topsoil with the subsoil to reduce the fertility. If you have a thin and chalky or light and sandy topsoil, then there should be no problem because the grass will grow more slowly and so the wild flowers will be able to compete more successfully.

WHERE TO PLACE YOUR MEADOW

In most gardens an area of mown grass is a necessity, as a space for relaxation, for children's play or to form a calm, still centre to the brightly coloured surrounding beds and borders, but in many cases there may be space to have a lawn close to the house and then to have an area of grass meadow beyond. Mown grass paths around or through the meadow will allow access to the meadow and to other garden areas beyond. The site needs to be sunny but it does not need to be very large, just enough to allow room for a good variety of grasses and wild flowers. Suitable grasses are described in the directory, as are a range of wild flowers, the best of which are listed in the box opposite.

CARING FOR A WILDFLOWER MEADOW

Your new meadow will need some care and attention. To start with, it will need mowing – first in spring before the wild flowers start growing and then again after the plants have flowered and set seed. All grass clippings need to be removed because they will smother new young plants and cause them to die. Never add fertilizer because this will only encourage the grass to grow more vigorously, which will stifle the wild flowers. To add early spring interest to your meadow, plant some bulbs like snowdrops and wild daffodils. If you are starting with an existing lawn, these bulbs can be planted in autumn, either before or after adding the wild flowers, although snowdrops in particular are best planted in spring as plants 'in the green' rather than as bulbs. If sowing a meadow from seed, you need to allow the meadow at least a year to get established before adding the bulbs.

LEFT *Create a mown path in the meadow to lead you through its delights and on into other areas of the garden. The path need not be straight – in fact for a natural feel it should meander.*

TECHNIQUE **PROPAGATING WILD FLOWERS**

1 Sow the wildflower seeds in seed trays in early spring. Place them where they will get light and warmth to encourage them to germinate.

2 Prick the seedlings out into small pots or seed trays when they are large enough to handle. Hold the plants by their leaves, not their roots, and use a 'widger' to make the hole.

3 Mow the grass, and plant out the small plants into the turf. Position them in a random pattern for a natural look, otherwise they will appear too regimented.

PROJECT **CREATING A NEW WILDFLOWER MEADOW**

STAR PLANTS

1 Check the soil fertility and remove topsoil if necessary, digging subsoil in with topsoil during the winter. In spring, prepare a tilth by breaking down any clods with a fork; rake the ground until it is level.

2 Firm the site by walking over it with your feet, using small steps with your weight on your heels. As the earth gets compacted you may notice some unevenness in the surface; rake the soil again for a level finish.

- *Anthyllis vulneraria* (kidney vetch)
- *Campanula rotundifolia* (harebell)
- *Galium verum* (lady's bedstraw)
- *Hippocrepis comosa* (horseshoe vetch)
- *Leucanthemum vulgare* (ox-eye daisy)
- *Linaria vulgaris* (toadflax)
- *Lotus corniculatus* (bird's-foot trefoil)
- *Primula veris* (cowslip)
- *Succisa pratensis* (Devil's bit scabious)

3 Rake over the soil to get a fine tilth on the surface. Leave for a week or two, so that any perennial weeds grow through. These should be removed.

4 Sow a mixture of wild flowers and grasses, scattering the seed on the surface as evenly as possible. You may find it easier to mix the seed with fine sand.

5 Rake over the surface to partially cover the seed. If birds start feeding on the seed, criss-cross the bed with fine thread. Water with a fine rose in very dry weather.

WATER AND WETLAND

*C*reating *a water and wetland area is one of the quickest ways to attract wildlife into your garden. Dig a pond and almost immediately the water will become home to beetles, water snails and water boatmen. Add a boggy area of planting nearby and frogs and toads will appear to lay their eggs in the pond and take up residence nearby. A pond also allows the introduction of yellow water iris, purple loosestrife and meadowsweet.*

It is worth taking a little time to plan your pond rather than just digging a hole, lining it and filling it with water. First find the right site. Water is normally found in low-lying areas, so look for a low point in the garden; you should ideally choose a place where there is a background of a hedge or shrubs so that animals can approach the water under cover of planting. Select a sunny, sheltered site on level ground, if possible, away from overhanging trees, which will quickly fill up the pond with leaves in autumn, to the detriment of its inhabitants. If there are small children in the family, consider the possibility of fencing off the pond at least until the children are old enough for the open water not to be a safety problem.

LEFT *The area beside a pond can be used as a bog garden for growing moisture-loving plants that would not survive elsewhere in the garden. Frogs and toads should also appear.*

STAR PLANTS FOR PONDS
❧ *Butomus umbellatus* (flowering rush) – marginal
❧ *Filipendula ulmaria* (meadowsweet) – bog garden
❧ *Iris pseudacorus* (yellow water iris) – marginal and bog garden
❧ *Lythrum salicaria* (purple loosestrife) – marginal
❧ *Mentha aquatica* (water mint) – marginal
❧ *Menyanthes trifoliata* (bog bean) – marginal
❧ *Nymphaea alba* (white water lily) – aquatic
❧ *Parnassia palustris* (grass of parnassus) – bog garden
❧ *Sagittaria sagittifolia* (arrow head) – marginal
❧ *Valeriana officinalis* (valerian) – bog garden

Make the pond as large as space will allow and design gently sloping sides for easy access by birds and mammals to the water's edge. The centre of the pond should be at least 75cm (30in) deep in order to prevent the pond freezing solid in winter or overheating in the summer.

Many preformed rigid ponds have very steep sides and are not really suitable for wildlife, so it is more sensible to create your pond using a flexible liner (*see opposite*).

AFTERCARE

Any new body of water will attract algae – small organisms that cover the surface with an ugly greenish 'blanketweed'. Planting the pond will help to control algae, since the plants will compete with the algae for light and nutrients. The algae may take control to begin with, but avoid using chemicals and allow the plants to do the job. This may mean physically removing some of the algae in the first season.

POND LIFE

Water beetles, water snails and other pond life will arrive of its own accord, although you may wish to import a few snails as a start. Many pond-owners will wish to include some fish, and these will have to be brought in from outside sources such as friends' ponds or pet stores. A wildlife pond should be stocked with native fish. Some species of stickle-backs and minnow are small enough to enjoy living in a garden pond and feeding on small insects, including mosquito larvae, and algae. Be careful if you want gold-fish because they are carnivorous and love eating tadpoles and other smaller pond inhabitants.

PROJECT | **MAKING A WILDLIFE POND USING A LINER**

1 Mark out the shape of the pond on the ground, including any areas that are to be used for bog plants.

2 Remove the surface vegetation. If this is grass, lift carefully so that it can be used elsewhere in the garden.

3 Carefully remove all the topsoil and store it somewhere out of the way, for re-use later.

4 Put in a datum peg at the level of the finished pond, then add pegs around the edge. Use a spirit-level and board to ensure the pegs are level.

5 Dig out the subsoil to create the pond, allowing for slopes and shelves as planned. Remove any stones.

6 Cover the base, sides and shelves with sand or fibre matting to protect the liner from being punctured by any remaining stones in the subsoil.

7 Lay the liner over the hole, pulling it taut and placing stones on the edge to hold it in position. Make sure that the overlap is evenly distributed.

8 Gradually fill the liner with water, using a hosepipe, so that it stretches to fit the shape of the hole. This may take quite a long time.

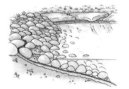

9 Cover the edges of the pond with gravel or stones for a sloping beach, paving for a viewing area and soil for any plant-growing areas.

10 Place a row of stones to define the edge of the bog garden, and then fill the area beyond with topsoil, concealing the edges of the liner.

11 Top up the water level and add containers of aquatic, oxygenating and marginal plants; place floating plants on the surface of the pond.

12 Plant up any wetland or bog areas around the pond with suitable plants.

THE FLOWER BORDER

A*flower border is not a natural habitat but a garden feature, and it can be planted to provide plenty of food for wildlife and to act as a refuge for several of the more attractive wild flowers. Many cultivated non-native garden flowers are rich in nectar and provide food for bees, bumblebees and butterflies, and as a result many of our gardens, planted with no thoughts of attracting wildlife, are full of bees and butterflies.*

Flowering plants are best placed in full sun if you want them to attract the maximum number of bees and butterflies. Choose a sheltered, sunny site that can be easily viewed from the house or patio. Flower borders normally consist of a mixture of native and non-native plants. Most gardeners want to include their favourite flowers in a border, and do not worry whether they are native or introduced. If planting for bees and butterflies, choose single-flowered cultivars, because the design of these blooms makes it easier for the insects to reach the nectar.

You can, however, plan a border using just plants that are native to your local area. For example, the following

scheme can be particularly effective for slightly damp soils: grow *Cardamine pratensis* (lady's smock), *Lychnis flos-cuculi* (ragged robin) and *Saponaria officinalis* (soapwort) in the front of the border, and *Filipendula ulmaria* (meadowsweet), *Eupatorium cannabinum* (hemp agrimony) and *Lythrum salicaria* (purple loosestrife) at the back. All these suggested plants prefer a fertile, well-drained soil. A native border always looks more natural with a hedge or shrubs as a backdrop, rather than a brick or stone wall, which makes it look more formal.

ENDANGERED PLANTS

There are several species of wild flower that are now so rare in the wild that they are protected by law, making it illegal either to pick the flowers or to dig up the plants in the wild. Some of these, however, make excellent garden plants, including *Dianthus gratianopolitanus* (Cheddar pink) – a lovely plant of limestone areas, but one that is easy to cultivate in well-drained alkaline soil. Many such rare and endangered plants can be legally obtained by gardeners from specialist nurseries, and it could be very rewarding to plant a bed or beds with endangered plants and so create your own wildflower refuge. In this way, you will also be helping in the conservation of the species. Check which plants are likely to grow in your soil by contacting your local conservation group and be sure to get plants or seed from a guaranteed local source.

ABOVE *Ornamental flowering plants can be used to attract bees and butterflies to any garden, but for butterflies to stay you will need to supply their caterpillars with food too.*

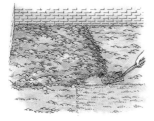

1 After making a planting plan, mark out the area to be planted and clear any existing vegetation by forking out all the roots. Spread a layer of compost over the area and lightly fork it into the topsoil. You are now ready to plant.

2 Check the compost around your chosen plants for moisture. If it feels quite dry, place the pots in a bucket of water to soak overnight before planting. Remove any weeds that are growing on the surface of the compost at the top of the pots.

3 Place the plants on the soil, following the plan, and check their spacing. First plant the buddleja and hebe, making sure that the planting holes are large enough for their roots and that the top of the root ball is completely covered.

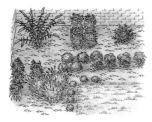

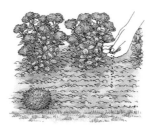

4 Next, add the herbaceous plants, such as Michaelmas daisies, ice plant and lavender, planting them firmly in their new positions within the plan.

5 The candytuft is a hardy annual and should be sown directly on to the soil where it is to flower in either autumn or spring. You will need to sow fresh seed each year. Water all plants well after planting.

STAR PLANTS

- *Aster novi-belgii* (Michaelmas daisy)
- *Aubrieta deltoidea*
- *Buddleja davidii* (butterfly bush)
- *Centranthus ruber* (red valerian)
- *Hebe salicifolia* (shrubby veronica)
- *Iberis amara* (candytuft)
- *Lavandula angustifolia* (lavender)
- *Origanum vulgare* (marjoram)
- *Sedum spectabile* (ice plant)
- *Tagetes patula* (French marigold)

BUTTERFLIES

Butterflies and moths are closely related. Butterflies have clubbed ends to their antennae whereas moth antennae are pointed. The adult butterflies fly by day, seeking nectar, whereas moths usually fly after dark (see *page 56*). When butterflies mate, the female lays her eggs either on or beside the appropriate food plant for the larva stage – the caterpillar. When the caterpillars are large enough, they pupate and the adults emerge. Common butterflies that may be seen in gardens are peacocks, red admirals, small tortoiseshells and cabbage whites (see *pages 32–3*).

Butterflies will visit any garden where there is a range of nectar-rich plants, provided that they are able to breed in the area. For this to occur, they are dependent on a good supply of the particular food plants on which their larvae feed. Caterpillars, however, are very specific about their food plants: many will feed on only a single species of plant and most diet on just a few closely related plants.

Planting a range of caterpillar food plants will ensure that you can enjoy watching the adult butterflies, which are less fussy and happy to visit a wide range of both ornamental and native plants for nectar.

THE HERB GARDEN

A herb garden is not strictly a habitat and is not usually planted with wildlife in mind, but many common herbs are excellent plants in this respect, being rich in nectar and so attracting bees, butterflies, hoverflies and other insects. Thyme and winter savory will be alive with bees throughout the summer, whereas lavender and marjoram also attract bees and many lovely butterflies. Angelica and fennel play host to many different insects, and the seed-eating birds relish angelica seeds in the autumn. Almost all herbs attract wildlife of some sort or another, so every garden should have its patch.

Herbs are useful plants that people have enjoyed for over 3,000 years. Their benefits are not confined simply to flavouring food, although for many of us that is their main use: they are also used to preserve food, to enhance the atmosphere and cloak noxious smells, to prepare cosmetics and to treat the sick. Many common herbs were cultivated by the ancient Romans, and although not strictly native

plants they have long been naturalized. Herbs contain essential oils within the cells of their leaves, stems and flowers, and it is these that give them their therapeutic value and flavour. Unlike scented flowers, however, the aroma is not always readily detectable, and in some herbs the leaves need to be chopped, crushed or cooked for the scent to emerge.

GROWING REQUIREMENTS

When planning a herb garden it is important to realize that herbs are grown together because it is convenient for the grower to have them all in one place. This does not mean that they all enjoy the same growing conditions and will happily thrive together in the same bed. In fact some, like rosemary, lavender and thyme, need a dry, sunny site, others, such as mint and *Levisticum officinale* (lovage), prefer a moist fertile soil, and others are happy in shade or partial shade, like angelica and *Myrrhis odorata* (sweet cicely). To try to accommodate these different require-ments, a herb garden is frequently divided into several beds, which allows some areas to have added compost and manure to keep the soil moist and fertile, whereas other areas are left unfed (a well-drained, neutral to slightly alka-line soil is the preferred home for many herbs).

PLANTING YOUR HERB GARDEN

Positioning the garden by the house has many benefits: the herbs can be readily picked for use, the bees can be viewed easily, and if you choose a site where the house wall shades part of the plot there will be both partially shaded beds and others in full sun. A 2m (6ft) square can contain all the herbs you are likely to need. Choose a dry day in mid to late spring to plant your herb garden.

ABOVE *It is a sensible idea to separate different areas of the herb garden for growing plants with similar requirements. Here a raised bed has been created by using woven wicker.*

HERBS IN CONTAINERS

A group of terracotta pots filled with fragrant, healthy herbs is a pleasure to see, and the different growing requirements of many herbs make it sensible to grow them in containers: the soil and drainage can be adjusted to suit each occupant and the containers can be placed in sun or shade according to each plant's preference. The pots can be placed near the house for ease of access and so that any visiting wildlife can be viewed from the windows. Two further advantages to growing herbs in pots are that rampant plants like mint, which could otherwise take over a plot, can be constrained, and that any herb that has been harvested and now needs time to rebuild its strength can be placed out of the way until it recovers.

STAR HERBS FOR WILDLIFE

- *Allium schoenoprasum* (chives) – bees and butterflies
- *Angelica archangelica* – bees, butterflies, hoverflies, insects, birds
- *Borago officinalis* (borage) – bees
- *Foeniculum vulgare* (fennel) – bees, hoverflies, caterpillars
- *Hyssopus officinalis* (hyssop) – lacewings and bees
- *Lavandula angustifolia* (lavender) – bees and butterflies
- *Mentha spicata* (spearmint) – bees, butterflies and moths
- *Origanum vulgare* (marjoram) – bees and butterflies
- *Rosmarinus officinalis* (rosemary) – bees, butterflies and hoverflies
- *Satureja montana* (winter savory) – bees
- *Thymus vulgaris* (thyme) – bees and butterflies

PROJECT — PLANTING A HERB GARDEN FOR BEES

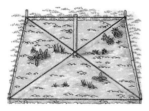

1 Mark out the area for your herb garden, making sure that it is square by checking the diagonals. Mark the centre point with a stake. You do not need a large area: 2 x 2m (6 x 6ft) is usually sufficient.

2 Remove all weeds from the marked area and lightly fork over the soil. Herbs are usually better in a less fertile soil, but you will need to add compost or manure for those herbs that favour these conditions.

3 Place a sundial in the centre of the garden, setting it on a paving slab in the exact centre. Using the sundial as the focal point of your design, you can now plan the planting scheme for your herbs.

4 Place the herbs in their pots in their allocated spaces, checking that the spacings look right and that the planting does not appear to be too regimented.

5 Start in the centre and carefully plant the plants, firming them in well. After planting, fork gently between the plants. Water well, using a fine rose.

6 For a less formal effect, scatter a packet of borage seed in the spaces between the herbs. Once these have flowered, allow them to self-seed for continued growth.

SECRET PLACES

*E*very wildlife garden needs some secret places where animals can hide away from humans and other predators, where they can sleep at night, produce young and hibernate in winter. Most gardens have odd corners where useful odds and ends accumulate, heaps of wood which will come in useful one day, an assortment of old terracotta flower pots too potentially valuable to discard, a roll of netting with holes that the rabbits get through, or a pile of leaves supposedly making leaf mould. Luckily most of us leave these alone, and they become home to insects and make nesting sites for robins, mice, hedgehogs and even snakes.

Secret places where wildlife can hide and nest range from undisturbed piles of logs or leaves to inviting patches of *Urtica dioica* (stinging nettles) or *Rubus fruticosus* (brambles). A compost heap will also provide such a refuge, as well as creating rich organic matter to help improve soil condition throughout the garden.

A LOG PILE

A 'forgotten' pile of logs makes a useful site for insects, spiders, ants and slugs, some of which live on decaying timber; others may use it as a hiding place. If the pile is situated in a damp location, it may even offer shelter to a toad. If you are going to create a log pile, choose a shady

STAR PLANTS FOR SMALL MAMMALS
Corylus avellana (hazel)
Crataegus monogyna (hawthorn)
Fagus sylvatica (beech)
Fragaria vesca (wild strawberry)
Malus domestica (apple)
Prunus domestica (plum)
Quercus robur (oak)
Rosa canina (dog rose)
Rubus fruticosus (bramble)
Rubus idaeus (raspberry)
Sorbus aucuparia (rowan)

place where the timber will not dry out too quickly, and you should ideally have a mixture of different timbers and a range of log sizes within the pile. Fungi which feed on decaying timber will quickly colonize the pile, followed by most of the insects, including solitary bees looking for nests. Predatory birds like wrens and blackbirds will then come looking for the insects. If the log pile is near the garden shed, the inhabitants can be watched from the windows without disturbance.

PILES OF LEAVES

A pile of leaves and garden prunings makes a welcome home for hedgehogs; but, before removing the leaves to put on a winter bonfire, do remember that they may be hibernating in the middle of the heap.

LEFT *A log pile will quickly become home to a wide variety of insects and spiders. These in turn will attract insectivorous birds which will come for the fresh food on offer.*

MAKING AN ORGANIC COMPOST HEAP

1 Site the heap out of direct sun, away from trees, and on bare soil or grass so that soil organisms can get in. Start with a layer of coarse material, such as cabbage leaves, to allow air into the base of the heap.

2 Fill up the first 15cm (6in) with kitchen waste, annual weeds and grass clippings. Add some soil and nitrogenous waste or organic fertilizer to encourage the composting process to begin.

3 Add another 15cm (6in) of mixed waste and activating matter. Continue creating layers until full. If dry, water the heap and cover it with old carpet or newspaper to stop it getting too wet when it rains.

4 Leave the heap, checking it is still moist if the weather is dry. After six weeks, it should be turning into compost. When ready, remove the 'lid' and place uncomposted material at the base of your next heap.

NETTLE PATCHES

These are another important mini-habitat for the caterpillars of the small tortoiseshell, peacock, comma and red admiral butterflies. Stinging nettles are also excellent material for adding to the compost heap. To prevent the nettles becoming a nuisance, create an enclosed rooting area for them by sinking a large container in the ground before planting. The caterpillars prefer young nettle leaves and butterflies will appreciate the nettles being cut back in midsummer to provide food for second broods of caterpillars in late summer.

BRAMBLE PATCHES

If you have room, find a space to let a blackberry plant or two go wild; brambles are a valuable source of food for many creatures and provide an 'armoured' resting place for birds and small mammals within the tangled mass of stems. It is essential to keep brambles under control; old stems should be removed each year and any suckers escaping into other areas must be ruthlessly eradicated.

THE COMPOST HEAP

All gardens need at least one compost heap so that garden and kitchen waste can be turned into organic matter to add to the soil in beds and borders (*see above*). The bacteria

HINTS AND TIPS FOR COMPOSTING

🐞 When making compost, if you have room in your garden try operating a system of three heaps – one for filling, one for leaving to break down into compost, and one that is ready for use in the garden.

🐞 Grass clippings, most prunings, annual flowers and vegetable peelings are all suitable for composting.

🐞 Always mix up items to be composted, so that air can circulate more freely.

🐞 To 'activate' the heap, use nitrogenous waste such as animal manure or an organic fertilizer such as seaweed meal, available from garden centres.

🐞 Some waste is unsuitable for composting: this includes anything that has been cooked, prunings from woody plants, diseased material, and weed seeds.

that break down the waste matter need nitrogen, heat, water and oxygen, and given the right balance they will rapidly multiply and create compost.

It is important to get the balance right between compacting the material in the heap to create heat and leaving it open enough for oxygen from the air to get in. You also need to make sure that there is sufficient moisture without drowning the bacteria. The heap will provide a secret place for wildlife, especially mice and voles.

THE WILD GARDEN AT NIGHT

Enter your garden at night and you will find yourself in a world full of secretive noises and darting flights. If you are lucky, you will see bats flitting silently past in the last of the evening light, and as the light fades the ghostly shadows of moths will be drawn to the light of an uncurtained window. Listen for the grunting of a hedgehog rummaging in the grass for slugs and snails, or the rattle of foxes raiding dustbins in search of easy food. High up, owls may hoot in the still of the night, and at your feet a veritable army of nocturnal insects and small mammals will be busy searching for food.

Many insects, including stag beetles, millipedes and earwigs, emerge at night when it is cooler and the darkness makes them less obvious to their predators. For similar reasons, slugs, snails, woodlice and earthworms are also nocturnal. Mammals, such as hedgehogs and badgers, that feed on these night-time wanderers have, therefore, adapted to a nocturnal way of life in order to exploit the potential midnight feast. Some of the smaller nocturnal mammals, like wood mice and dormice, are nocturnal feeders and so are, in turn, food for the owls hunting at night.

MOTHS
Moths are related to butterflies and share the same life cycle: the adult moths feed on nectar, mate and then lay their eggs on the food plant of the larva or caterpillar. When

FOOD PLANTS FOR LARGER MOTHS

- *Epilobium angustifolium* (rosebay willowherb) – elephant hawk-moth
- *Galium verum* (lady's bedstraw) – humming bird, bedstraw, bee and elephant hawk-moths
- *Ligustrum vulgare* (privet) – privet hawk-moth
- *Lonicera periclymenum* (honeysuckle) – bee hawk-moth
- *Malus sylvestris* (crab apple) – eyed hawk-moth
- *Pinus sylvestris* (Scots pine) – pine hawk-moth
- *Populus nigra* (black poplar) – poplar hawk-moth, puss moth
- *Prunus spinosa* (sloe) – emperor moth
- *Salix cinerea* (grey sallow) – puss moth, sallow kitten, swallow prominent
- *Tilia cordata* (lime) – lime hawk-moth

it is large enough, the caterpillar pupates and the adult moth emerges. Most moths rest by day and start flying to find nectar in the evening. The largest and most dramatic are the hawk-moths, many of which are now rarely seen, but the elephant, lime and privet hawk-moths frequently visit gardens at night to feed on honeysuckle.

NIGHT-SCENTED PLANTS
There are a number of delightful plants that have flowers which open at the end of the day and stay open into the night. Many of them are scented; the fragrance attracts moths for nectar and thereby ensures that the flowers are pollinated. Moths are attracted by white or light-coloured

LEFT *Owls are perhaps the most exciting night-time visitors to our gardens. The distinctive call of the tawny owl is one of the great pleasures of summer evenings.*

flowers, which tend to glow in the pale evening light; for this reason, night-scented flowers are usually white, cream, yellow or pale pink. To grow night-scented plants, select a sheltered site by the house, and near a window, so that when they are established you can watch the moths visiting the flowers without disturbing them, although it is also pleasant to sit outside and enjoy the evening fragrance yourself. The plants recommended for attracting moths (*see right*) usually prefer a fertile, well-drained soil.

BATS

Bats fly in the evening and night, feeding mostly on moths and beetles, so the more moths you attract into the garden the greater the likelihood of attracting bats. If you want to have resident bats then you need to provide roosting sites for nesting and hibernating. Your local bat group should be

PLANTS FOR ATTRACTING MOTHS

- *Centranthus ruber* (red valerian)
- *Hesperis matronalis* (sweet rocket)
- *Jasminum officinale* (jasmine)
- *Lonicera periclymenum* (honeysuckle)
- *Matthiola longipetala* subsp. *bicornis* (night-scented stock)
- *Nicotiana alata* (tobacco plant)
- *Oenothera biennis* (evening primrose)
- *Phlox paniculata*
- *Saponaria officinalis* (soapwort)
- *Silene vulgaris* (bladder campion)

consulted about bats in your area and about the most appropriate roosting sites and bat boxes. Bats are protected by law: it is illegal to destroy roosting sites or bat boxes.

PROJECT | PLANTING A CORNER BED FOR ATTRACTING MOTHS

1 Clear the area of weeds and then fork over the soil, digging in compost or well-rotted farmyard manure. You are then ready to plant (*see panel above right*).

2 Plant the honeysuckle and jasmine a little way away from the walls: the soil can be dry and infertile by a wall and the foundations may get in the way.

3 Place the rest of the plants in their pots on the soil to see whether they will have enough space. When you are happy with their position, remove them from the pots.

4 Plant the evening primroses at the back, allowing plenty of space for these self-seeding biennials. Then plant the phlox, sweet rocket and bladder campion.

5 If you have planted in early spring, rake the front of the border and sow seed of night-scented stock as an edging along the front of the border.

6 When all danger of frost is past, plant out the tobacco plants. These and the night-scented stock are annuals and so will need to be replaced each year.

THE
PLANT
DIRECTORY

The major attraction for wildlife in any garden is the range of plants, which provide insects, birds and small mammals with food and shelter. Such plants include the short-lived, colourful annuals and biennials, with their nectar and pollen that are loved by butterflies and bees, as well as shrubs and trees that provide homes for birds and squirrels. Other types of flowering and fruiting plants, such as herbaceous perennials, climbers, bulbs and herbs also help to create a welcoming environment.

LEFT. *This mixture of flowers and foliage clumps will attract insects for nectar as well as providing shelter and hiding places for wildlife.*

HOW TO USE THIS DIRECTORY

The Plant Directory lists all the plants that are featured in this book, together with a selection of other plants that are suitable for use in a wildlife garden. It is not intended to be exhaustive, and experienced gardeners will have their own favourites to add. This listing has, however, been made with the specific requirements of a wildlife garden in mind, and it will guide the beginner to a range of attractive and readily available plants, shrubs and trees with which to create a beautiful garden. Complete information on planting and maintaining the plants is given for each entry.

The Plant Directory is divided into different categories that group similar plants together. The categories are: annuals and biennials (*pages 62–7*), bulbs (*pages 68–9*), herbaceous perennials (*pages 70–83*), grasses and ferns (*pages 84–5*), shrubs (*pages 86–95*), climbers (*pages 96–7*), trees (*pages 98–103*) and herbs (*pages 104–7*).

The symbols panel accompanying each entry gives essential information on growing conditions (*see opposite page for a key to the symbols*). The text next to each colour photograph gives a brief description of the plant, indicates when flowering types are in bloom and explains what type of soil each plant prefers.

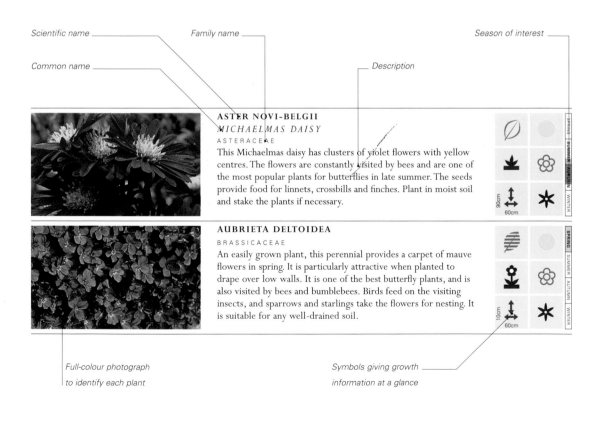

Scientific name

Common name

Family name

Description

Season of interest

ASTER NOVI-BELGII
MICHAELMAS DAISY
ASTERACEAE
This Michaelmas daisy has clusters of violet flowers with yellow centres. The flowers are constantly visited by bees and are one of the most popular plants for butterflies in late summer. The seeds provide food for linnets, crossbills and finches. Plant in moist soil and stake the plants if necessary.

AUBRIETA DELTOIDEA
BRASSICACEAE
An easily grown plant, this perennial provides a carpet of mauve flowers in spring. It is particularly attractive when planted to drape over low walls. It is one of the best butterfly plants, and is also visited by bees and bumblebees. Birds feed on the visiting insects, and sparrows and starlings take the flowers for nesting. It is suitable for any well-drained soil.

Full-colour photograph
to identify each plant

Symbols giving growth
information at a glance

KEY TO THE SYMBOLS

 EASY TO GROW

These are tolerant plants that require no special care or conditions in order to flourish.

 MODERATE TO GROW

These are plants that require some special care, such as protection from frost.

DIFFICULT TO GROW

These are plants that require a great deal of specialized care, and offer a challenge for the more experienced gardener.

EVERGREEN

SEMI-EVERGREEN

DECIDUOUS

Deciduous plants lose all their leaves in autumn (sometimes in summer) while evergreen plants keep their foliage all the year round. Plants described as semi-evergreen may keep some or all of their foliage through the winter in sheltered gardens or if the weather is mild. No leaf symbol is given for annuals, nor for biennials, although some biennials do keep their leaves over the first winter.

 **FEATURE LEAVES**

FEATURE SCENT

FEATURE FLOWER

FEATURE FRUIT

These symbols indicate the main feature of interest for each plant in the directory. This will help you to choose plants that have complementary features, or plants that will perform a specific function in your garden. The symbols show the main feature of interest, but this is not necessarily the plant's only attractive asset.

 RAPID GROWTH

 MODERATE GROWTH

 SLOW GROWTH

Speed of growth, like ease of growth, is a highly subjective category, and will vary according to local conditions. Rapid growth indicates plants that reach their full extent in a single season (annuals for instance), or plants that make substantial progress towards filling the space allowed for them in a single season. Slow growth indicates plants, such as trees and some shrubs, that take several seasons to reach their ultimate size. Moderate growth refers, therefore, to rates of progress between these two extremes.

The period of the year when a plant is likely to be at its most attractive is also indicated. This will allow you, for instance, to create a planting scheme that will have something of interest for each season of the year.

 HEIGHT AND SPREAD

The size of plants will vary according to the growing conditions in your garden, so these measurements are a rough guide only. In all cases the measurements refer to the size of plants and trees when mature, although again there are specific cases where the ultimate size is never reached. For instance, bedding and climbing roses can be pruned to fit smaller spaces, and the spread of water plants may be governed largely by the size of the pond they are planted in.

FULL SUN

PARTIAL SUN

SHADE

An indication of light preference is given to show each plant's optimum growing situation. Here again, this is only a rough guide, as some plants that prefer sun may also be reasonably tolerant of shade.

ANNUALS AND BIENNIALS

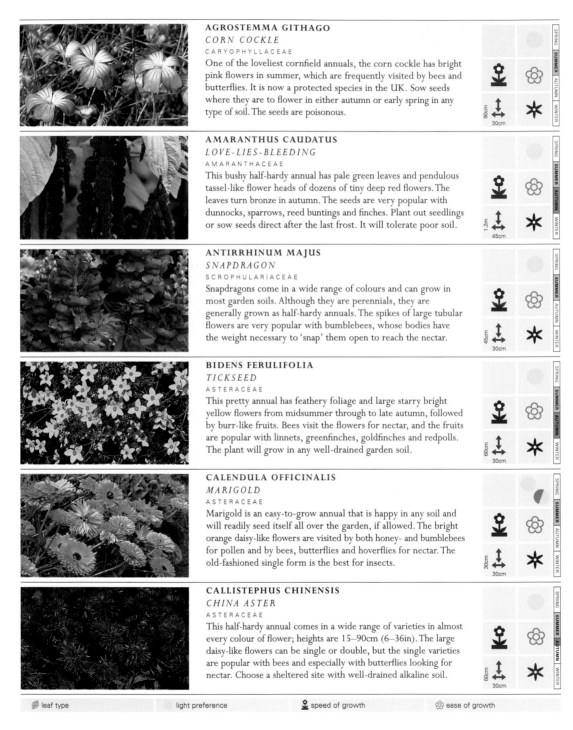

AGROSTEMMA GITHAGO
CORN COCKLE
CARYOPHYLLACEAE

One of the loveliest cornfield annuals, the corn cockle has bright pink flowers in summer, which are frequently visited by bees and butterflies. It is now a protected species in the UK. Sow seeds where they are to flower in either autumn or early spring in any type of soil. The seeds are poisonous.

AMARANTHUS CAUDATUS
LOVE-LIES-BLEEDING
AMARANTHACEAE

This bushy half-hardy annual has pale green leaves and pendulous tassel-like flower heads of dozens of tiny deep red flowers. The leaves turn bronze in autumn. The seeds are very popular with dunnocks, sparrows, reed buntings and finches. Plant out seedlings or sow seeds direct after the last frost. It will tolerate poor soil.

ANTIRRHINUM MAJUS
SNAPDRAGON
SCROPHULARIACEAE

Snapdragons come in a wide range of colours and can grow in most garden soils. Although they are perennials, they are generally grown as half-hardy annuals. The spikes of large tubular flowers are very popular with bumblebees, whose bodies have the weight necessary to 'snap' them open to reach the nectar.

BIDENS FERULIFOLIA
TICKSEED
ASTERACEAE

This pretty annual has feathery foliage and large starry bright yellow flowers from midsummer through to late autumn, followed by burr-like fruits. Bees visit the flowers for nectar, and the fruits are popular with linnets, greenfinches, goldfinches and redpolls. The plant will grow in any well-drained garden soil.

CALENDULA OFFICINALIS
MARIGOLD
ASTERACEAE

Marigold is an easy-to-grow annual that is happy in any soil and will readily seed itself all over the garden, if allowed. The bright orange daisy-like flowers are visited by both honey- and bumblebees for pollen and by bees, butterflies and hoverflies for nectar. The old-fashioned single form is the best for insects.

CALLISTEPHUS CHINENSIS
CHINA ASTER
ASTERACEAE

This half-hardy annual comes in a wide range of varieties in almost every colour of flower; heights are 15–90cm (6–36in). The large daisy-like flowers can be single or double, but the single varieties are popular with bees and especially with butterflies looking for nectar. Choose a sheltered site with well-drained alkaline soil.

| leaf type | light preference | speed of growth | ease of growth |

CENTAUREA CYANUS
CORNFLOWER
ASTERACEAE

The bright blue flowers of cornflower were once a familiar sight in the cornfields in summer. An easy-to-grow annual, it can be sown direct in autumn or spring in any well-drained soil. The flowers are visited by bees for pollen and nectar and by butterflies for nectar; the seeds are food for blue tits, finches, siskins and crossbills.

60cm
20cm

CHRYSANTHEMUM SEGETUM
CORN MARIGOLD
ASTERACEAE

A lovely annual weed of cornfields, with bright yellow daisy flowers above bushy green foliage, the corn marigold has almost been eradicated by weedkillers in the countryside. The flowers provide nectar and pollen for honeybees and butterflies. Sow with other cornfield annuals in well-drained soil.

45cm
20cm

DAHLIA COLTNESS HYBRIDS
ASTERACEAE

There are many different dahlias available and the Coltness hybrids are some of the best. A tuberous perennial grown as an annual, the plant has deeply lobed leaves and fleshy stems of daisy-like single flowers that flower right up until the first frost. It is popular with butterflies, including red admirals, and bees for both pollen and nectar. Grow in any well-drained fertile soil.

45cm
45cm

DIANTHUS BARBATUS
SWEET WILLIAM
CARYOPHYLLACEAE

Sweet William is a short-lived perennial usually grown as an annual or biennial. In late spring and early summer, large flat heads of pink, red or white flowers are produced; these are deliciously fragrant and very popular with butterflies and bumblebees seeking nectar. Grow in well-drained fertile soil.

45cm
30cm

DIGITALIS PURPUREA
FOXGLOVE
SCROPHULARIACEAE

One of the most striking wild plants, with tall spikes of pinky-purple flowers, foxgloves are happiest in moist, humus-rich soil under the canopy of trees. A biennial, the seed should be sown in late summer where it is to flower the next year. The flowers are visited by bumblebees. All parts of the plant are poisonous.

1.5m
45cm

DIPSACUS FULLONUM
TEASEL
DIPSACACEAE

Teasels are tall architectural biennial plants. The rosettes of bristly leaves are food for the larvae of the marsh fritillary butterfly. In the second summer, tall stems of mauve spiny flower heads provide nectar for bees and butterflies. Later the seeds attract goldfinches and crossbills. Grow in any soil including heavy clay.

2m
45cm

---

height and spread   feature of interest   season of interest   *ANNUALS AND BIENNIALS* **A – D**

ANNUALS AND BIENNIALS

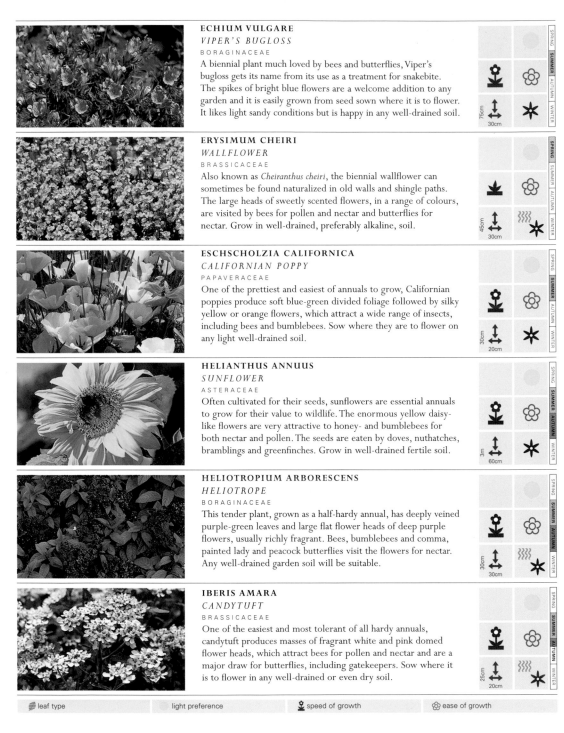

ECHIUM VULGARE
VIPER'S BUGLOSS
BORAGINACEAE

A biennial plant much loved by bees and butterflies, Viper's bugloss gets its name from its use as a treatment for snakebite. The spikes of bright blue flowers are a welcome addition to any garden and it is easily grown from seed sown where it is to flower. It likes light sandy conditions but is happy in any well-drained soil.

ERYSIMUM CHEIRI
WALLFLOWER
BRASSICACEAE

Also known as *Cheiranthus cheiri*, the biennial wallflower can sometimes be found naturalized in old walls and shingle paths. The large heads of sweetly scented flowers, in a range of colours, are visited by bees for pollen and nectar and butterflies for nectar. Grow in well-drained, preferably alkaline, soil.

ESCHSCHOLZIA CALIFORNICA
CALIFORNIAN POPPY
PAPAVERACEAE

One of the prettiest and easiest of annuals to grow, Californian poppies produce soft blue-green divided foliage followed by silky yellow or orange flowers, which attract a wide range of insects, including bees and bumblebees. Sow where they are to flower on any light well-drained soil.

HELIANTHUS ANNUUS
SUNFLOWER
ASTERACEAE

Often cultivated for their seeds, sunflowers are essential annuals to grow for their value to wildlife. The enormous yellow daisy-like flowers are very attractive to honey- and bumblebees for both nectar and pollen. The seeds are eaten by doves, nuthatches, bramblings and greenfinches. Grow in well-drained fertile soil.

HELIOTROPIUM ARBORESCENS
HELIOTROPE
BORAGINACEAE

This tender plant, grown as a half-hardy annual, has deeply veined purple-green leaves and large flat flower heads of deep purple flowers, usually richly fragrant. Bees, bumblebees and comma, painted lady and peacock butterflies visit the flowers for nectar. Any well-drained garden soil will be suitable.

IBERIS AMARA
CANDYTUFT
BRASSICACEAE

One of the easiest and most tolerant of all hardy annuals, candytuft produces masses of fragrant white and pink domed flower heads, which attract bees for pollen and nectar and are a major draw for butterflies, including gatekeepers. Sow where it is to flower in any well-drained or even dry soil.

| leaf type | light preference | speed of growth | ease of growth |

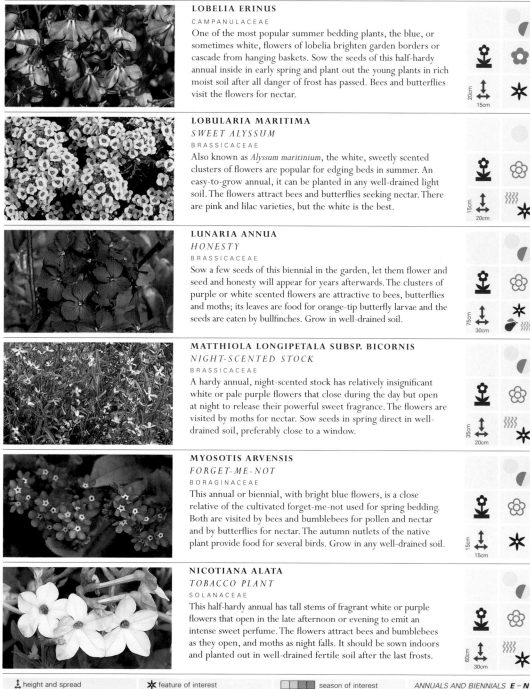

LOBELIA ERINUS
CAMPANULACEAE

One of the most popular summer bedding plants, the blue, or sometimes white, flowers of lobelia brighten garden borders or cascade from hanging baskets. Sow the seeds of this half-hardy annual inside in early spring and plant out the young plants in rich moist soil after all danger of frost has passed. Bees and butterflies visit the flowers for nectar.

20cm / 15cm

LOBULARIA MARITIMA
SWEET ALYSSUM
BRASSICACEAE

Also known as *Alyssum maritinium*, the white, sweetly scented clusters of flowers are popular for edging beds in summer. An easy-to-grow annual, it can be planted in any well-drained light soil. The flowers attract bees and butterflies seeking nectar. There are pink and lilac varieties, but the white is the best.

15cm / 20cm

LUNARIA ANNUA
HONESTY
BRASSICACEAE

Sow a few seeds of this biennial in the garden, let them flower and seed and honesty will appear for years afterwards. The clusters of purple or white scented flowers are attractive to bees, butterflies and moths; its leaves are food for orange-tip butterfly larvae and the seeds are eaten by bullfinches. Grow in well-drained soil.

75cm / 30cm

MATTHIOLA LONGIPETALA SUBSP. BICORNIS
NIGHT-SCENTED STOCK
BRASSICACEAE

A hardy annual, night-scented stock has relatively insignificant white or pale purple flowers that close during the day but open at night to release their powerful sweet fragrance. The flowers are visited by moths for nectar. Sow seeds in spring direct in well-drained soil, preferably close to a window.

35cm / 20cm

MYOSOTIS ARVENSIS
FORGET-ME-NOT
BORAGINACEAE

This annual or biennial, with bright blue flowers, is a close relative of the cultivated forget-me-not used for spring bedding. Both are visited by bees and bumblebees for pollen and nectar and by butterflies for nectar. The autumn nutlets of the native plant provide food for several birds. Grow in any well-drained soil.

15cm / 15cm

NICOTIANA ALATA
TOBACCO PLANT
SOLANACEAE

This half-hardy annual has tall stems of fragrant white or purple flowers that open in the late afternoon or evening to emit an intense sweet perfume. The flowers attract bees and bumblebees as they open, and moths as night falls. It should be sown indoors and planted out in well-drained fertile soil after the last frosts.

60cm / 30cm

↕ height and spread   ✳ feature of interest   ▭▭▭▭ season of interest   *ANNUALS AND BIENNIALS* **E – N**

ANNUALS AND BIENNIALS

OENOTHERA BIENNIS
EVENING PRIMROSE
ONAGRACEAE

Evening primrose is a biennial with tall spikes of soft yellow papery flowers arising from basal rosettes of leaves in the second summer. The scented flowers open in the evening, attracting late-flying bees for pollen and moths for nectar. The seeds are eaten by many birds. Sow in any well-drained soil.

ONOPORDUM ACANTHIUM
COTTON THISTLE
ASTERACEAE

A magnificent architectural biennial with large-lobed spiny silvery-grey leaves and tall erect grey winged stems. The deep purplish-pink flower heads are visited by bees for nectar and pollen. The seed heads provide food for birds, especially finches. Plant at the back of the border in a light well-drained soil.

PAPAVER RHOEAS
CORN POPPY
PAPAVERACEAE

This annual of waste ground and cornfields has large bright red papery flowers, followed by 'pepper pot' fruits. The seed falls to the ground, where it lies dormant until disturbed by cultivation. Hoverflies, bees, bumblebees and butterflies visit the flowers, and the seeds are eaten by birds. Sow in any well-drained soil.

PETUNIA HYBRIDS
SOLANACEAE

Petunias are half-hardy annuals that need to be sown indoors and planted outside when any danger of frost is past. The large funnel-shaped flowers are available in a wide range of colours and are visited by moths in the early evening. Petunias like hot, dry summers and may suffer in cold, wet weather. They will grow in any well-drained soil.

PHACELIA CAMPANULARIA
CALIFORNIAN BLUEBELL
HYDROPHYLLACEAE

This lovely hardy annual forms low domes of oval serrated deep green leaves and 2.5cm (1in) intense blue bell-shaped flowers, which are a favourite with bees for both pollen and nectar. Very fast-growing, it can be sown in autumn or spring where it is to flower and is happy in any well-drained garden soil.

RESEDA ODORATA
MIGNONETTE
RESEDACEAE

This hardy annual is grown for its intense spicy fragrance rather than for its untidy clusters of tiny greenish-yellow flowers. It is popular with bees seeking nectar and pollen and is also visited by butterflies. Select a variety like 'Sweet Scented' for maximum scent, and grow in any well-drained alkaline garden soil.

leaf type | light preference | speed of growth | ease of growth

SCABIOSA ATROPURPUREA
SWEET SCABIOUS
DIPSACACEAE

A hardy annual, this has large pincushion flower heads in a range of colours from white to blue, pink, lilac and red. The lightly scented flowers are popular with bees and painted lady, comma and peacock butterflies seeking nectar. It prefers a well-drained slightly alkaline soil and may suffer in prolonged wet weather.

60cm
30cm

SILYBUM MARIANUM
MILK THISTLE
ASTERACEAE

A spectacular biennial that produces tall pinky-purple flower heads in late summer, which are constantly visited by goldfinches in search of seeds. The milk-white veins on its spiny leaves give it its common name. Grow in well-drained soil and remove excess seedlings to avoid your garden being overrun.

1.5m
45cm

TAGETES ERECTA HYBRIDS
AFRICAN MARIGOLD
ASTERACEAE

One of the most popular flowers for butterflies, the bright yellow and orange African marigolds provide a bright splash of colour throughout the summer. A half-hardy annual, the seeds should be sown inside and the plants planted in well-drained soil after the last frosts. The flowers attract many butterflies.

45cm
30cm

TAGETES PATULA HYBRIDS
FRENCH MARIGOLD
ASTERACEAE

Smaller and more floriferous than *Tagetes erecta* hybrids, the half-hardy annual French marigolds attract a wide range of butterflies, including the common blue. The flowers also appeal to hoverflies, which feed on aphids on neighbouring plants and so provide a natural pest control. Grow in any well-drained soil.

30cm
20cm

VERBENA X HYBRIDA
VERBENACEAE

There are lots of different garden verbenas but these are the low-growing hybrid cultivars that are grown as half-hardy annuals. They have serrated deep green leaves and clusters of tubular flowers in pink, white, red, blue and mauve. They are popular with bees for both nectar and pollen and with butterflies for nectar. Grow in any well-drained soil.

25cm
30cm

ZINNIA ELEGANS
ASTERACEAE

Zinnias are half-hardy annuals and make lovely bedding plants, with their neat green foliage and large dahlia-like flowers in every colour except blue. They need well-drained soil and warm, dry summers in order to grow well, and regular dead-heading is necessary to ensure continual flowering. They are popular with bees for both nectar and pollen.

60cm
30cm

SPRING SUMMER AUTUMN WINTER

⬍ height and spread   ✳ feature of interest   ▮▮▮▮ season of interest   *ANNUALS AND BIENNIALS* **O – Z**

BULBS

ALLIUM GIGANTEUM
FLOWERING ONION
ALLIACEAE

This is perhaps the tallest and most spectacular of the many ornamental onions. The large 10cm (4in) wide globular heads of purple flowers appear in early summer and act as a magnet to bees, butterflies and other insects. Plant bulbs, at least 15cm (6in) deep, in the middle or back of the border, in well-drained soil.

COLCHICUM AUTUMNALE
AUTUMN CROCUS
COLCHICACEAE

Colchicums flower in the autumn after the bright shiny green leaves have died down. Tall goblet-shaped purple, pink or white flowers appear, which are visited by bees and bumblebees for nectar and pollen. Plant in autumn, 7.5cm (3in) deep, in a humus-rich, moist soil. All plant parts are poisonous.

CROCUS CHRYSANTHUS
IRIDACEAE

This spring-flowering crocus has cream or yellow flowers in early spring. On sunny spring days the flowers are visited by bees seeking pollen and nectar. One disadvantage is that the flower petals are often attacked by starlings and house sparrows, who leave them scattered all over the surrounding area. Plant corms in late autumn, 6cm (2½in) deep, in any well-drained soil.

ERANTHIS HYEMALIS
WINTER ACONITE
RANUNCULACEAE

Although botanically a tuber, winter aconite is usually treated as a bulb. Now naturalized in many parts of Britain, its bright yellow flowers appear in late winter and early spring and are visited by waking insects, including bees, for pollen. Plant tubers in late summer, 5cm (2in) deep, in humus-rich moist soil.

FRITILLARIA IMPERIALIS
CROWN IMPERIAL
LILIACEAE

Crown imperials have tall stems of glossy leaves with a head of bright orange pendulous bell flowers in spring; these provide nectar for blue tits, blackcaps, bees and bumblebees. Plant the large bulbs, at least 20cm (8in) deep, in well-drained fertile soil. Red- and yellow-flowered cultivars are available.

FRITILLARIA MELEAGRIS
SNAKESHEAD FRITILLARY
LILIACEAE

Now rare in the wild, snakeshead fritillary naturally grows in damp water meadows, where its pink-and-purple chequered flowers bloom in mid- to late spring. The flowers provide nectar for early butterflies and other insects. Plant bulbs, 10cm (4in) deep, in late autumn in damp fertile soil in either borders or grass areas.

| leaf type | light preference | speed of growth | ease of growth |

GALANTHUS NIVALIS
SNOWDROP
AMARYLLIDACEAE

One of the first flowers to appear, the snowdrop reminds us that winter is nearly over and spring is on the way. The flowers provide nectar for insects, including bees emerging prematurely from winter hibernation. Plant bulbs in autumn, 5cm (2in) deep, in rich moist soil in drifts under shrubs and trees.

HYACINTHOIDES NON-SCRIPTA
BLUEBELL
HYACINTHACEAE

The bluebell, with its typical hanging blue flowers, is found covering the ground in open woodland in spring. Plant groups of bulbs under trees in the garden in humus-rich soil. Plant in early autumn, 10–15cm (4–6in) deep, and leave undisturbed. The flowers are visited by several insects including some bees and butterflies.

HYACINTHUS ORIENTALIS
HYACINTHACEAE

Hyacinths are one of the best flowering bulbs for scent, the tightly packed flower heads producing a wonderful sweet fragrance. There are numerous cultivars, which come in a range of colours, but blue is usually the most popular. They are visited by bees for pollen and nectar. Plant the bulbs in autumn, 15cm (6in) deep, in well-drained fertile soil.

MUSCARI ARMENIACUM
GRAPE HYACINTH
HYACINTHACEAE

Grape hyacinths are among the easiest of bulbs to grow and they self-seed readily around the garden. The clusters of bright blue flowers appear in spring and attract tortoiseshell and brimstone butterflies as well as bees to feed on their nectar. Plant the bulbs in autumn, 7.5cm (3in) deep, in any soil.

NARCISSUS PSEUDONARCISSUS
DAFFODIL
AMARYLLIDACEAE

The wild daffodil, or lent lily, is smaller and less flamboyant than its cultivated cousins but still a most attractive plant for naturalizing in grass and under trees in gardens. Plant bulbs in late autumn, at least 7.5cm (3in) deep, in any ordinary garden soil. When clumps become too crowded, lift and divide after flowering.

TULIPA KAUFMANNIANA
WATER LILY TULIP
LILIACEAE

This is one of the loveliest of the early-flowering tulips, with short red-and-cream striped flowers and greyish-green leaves, which are frequently mottled. The flowers are visited by bees and bumblebees for pollen. Plant bulbs, at least 15cm (6in) deep, in well-drained fertile soil where they can be left undisturbed.

⥮ height and spread   ✳ feature of interest   ▭▭▭ season of interest   *BULBS* **A – T**

HERBACEOUS PERENNIALS

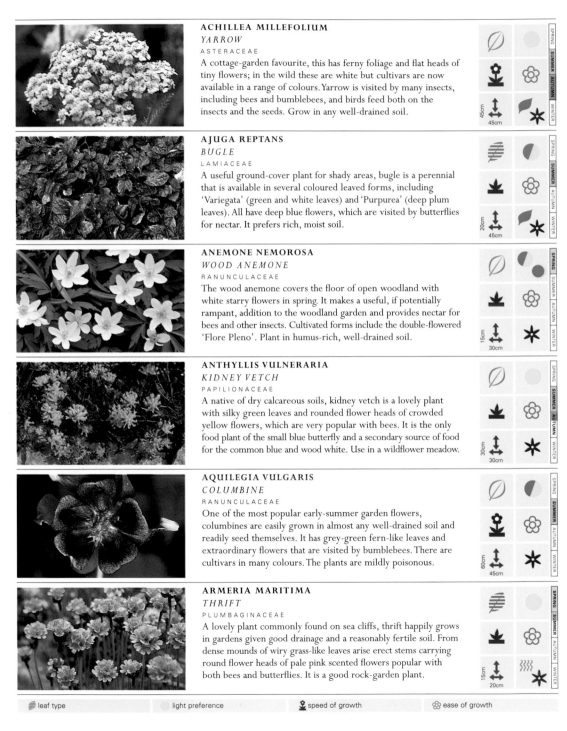

ACHILLEA MILLEFOLIUM
YARROW
ASTERACEAE

A cottage-garden favourite, this has ferny foliage and flat heads of tiny flowers; in the wild these are white but cultivars are now available in a range of colours. Yarrow is visited by many insects, including bees and bumblebees, and birds feed both on the insects and the seeds. Grow in any well-drained soil.

AJUGA REPTANS
BUGLE
LAMIACEAE

A useful ground-cover plant for shady areas, bugle is a perennial that is available in several coloured leaved forms, including 'Variegata' (green and white leaves) and 'Purpurea' (deep plum leaves). All have deep blue flowers, which are visited by butterflies for nectar. It prefers rich, moist soil.

ANEMONE NEMOROSA
WOOD ANEMONE
RANUNCULACEAE

The wood anemone covers the floor of open woodland with white starry flowers in spring. It makes a useful, if potentially rampant, addition to the woodland garden and provides nectar for bees and other insects. Cultivated forms include the double-flowered 'Flore Pleno'. Plant in humus-rich, well-drained soil.

ANTHYLLIS VULNERARIA
KIDNEY VETCH
PAPILIONACEAE

A native of dry calcareous soils, kidney vetch is a lovely plant with silky green leaves and rounded flower heads of crowded yellow flowers, which are very popular with bees. It is the only food plant of the small blue butterfly and a secondary source of food for the common blue and wood white. Use in a wildflower meadow.

AQUILEGIA VULGARIS
COLUMBINE
RANUNCULACEAE

One of the most popular early-summer garden flowers, columbines are easily grown in almost any well-drained soil and readily seed themselves. It has grey-green fern-like leaves and extraordinary flowers that are visited by bumblebees. There are cultivars in many colours. The plants are mildly poisonous.

ARMERIA MARITIMA
THRIFT
PLUMBAGINACEAE

A lovely plant commonly found on sea cliffs, thrift happily grows in gardens given good drainage and a reasonably fertile soil. From dense mounds of wiry grass-like leaves arise erect stems carrying round flower heads of pale pink scented flowers popular with both bees and butterflies. It is a good rock-garden plant.

🍃 leaf type   ● light preference   ⚘ speed of growth   ⚘ ease of growth

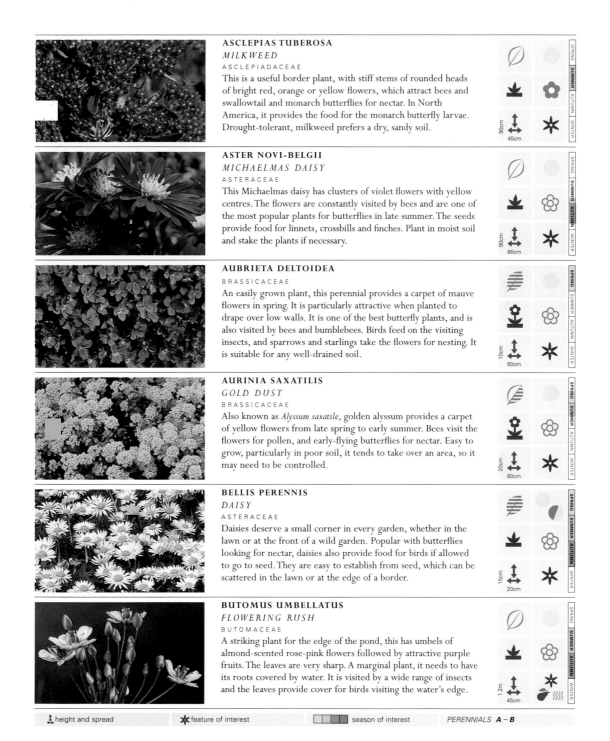

ASCLEPIAS TUBEROSA
MILKWEED
ASCLEPIADACEAE

This is a useful border plant, with stiff stems of rounded heads of bright red, orange or yellow flowers, which attract bees and swallowtail and monarch butterflies for nectar. In North America, it provides the food for the monarch butterfly larvae. Drought-tolerant, milkweed prefers a dry, sandy soil.

90cm / 45cm

ASTER NOVI-BELGII
MICHAELMAS DAISY
ASTERACEAE

This Michaelmas daisy has clusters of violet flowers with yellow centres. The flowers are constantly visited by bees and are one of the most popular plants for butterflies in late summer. The seeds provide food for linnets, crossbills and finches. Plant in moist soil and stake the plants if necessary.

90cm / 60cm

AUBRIETA DELTOIDEA
BRASSICACEAE

An easily grown plant, this perennial provides a carpet of mauve flowers in spring. It is particularly attractive when planted to drape over low walls. It is one of the best butterfly plants, and is also visited by bees and bumblebees. Birds feed on the visiting insects, and sparrows and starlings take the flowers for nesting. It is suitable for any well-drained soil.

10cm / 60cm

AURINIA SAXATILIS
GOLD DUST
BRASSICACEAE

Also known as *Alyssum saxatile*, golden alyssum provides a carpet of yellow flowers from late spring to early summer. Bees visit the flowers for pollen, and early-flying butterflies for nectar. Easy to grow, particularly in poor soil, it tends to take over an area, so it may need to be controlled.

20cm / 60cm

BELLIS PERENNIS
DAISY
ASTERACEAE

Daisies deserve a small corner in every garden, whether in the lawn or at the front of a wild garden. Popular with butterflies looking for nectar, daisies also provide food for birds if allowed to go to seed. They are easy to establish from seed, which can be scattered in the lawn or at the edge of a border.

15cm / 20cm

BUTOMUS UMBELLATUS
FLOWERING RUSH
BUTOMACEAE

A striking plant for the edge of the pond, this has umbels of almond-scented rose-pink flowers followed by attractive purple fruits. The leaves are very sharp. A marginal plant, it needs to have its roots covered by water. It is visited by a wide range of insects and the leaves provide cover for birds visiting the water's edge.

1.2m / 45cm

⬍ height and spread ✳ feature of interest ▢▢▢▢ season of interest *PERENNIALS A – B*

HERBACEOUS PERENNIALS

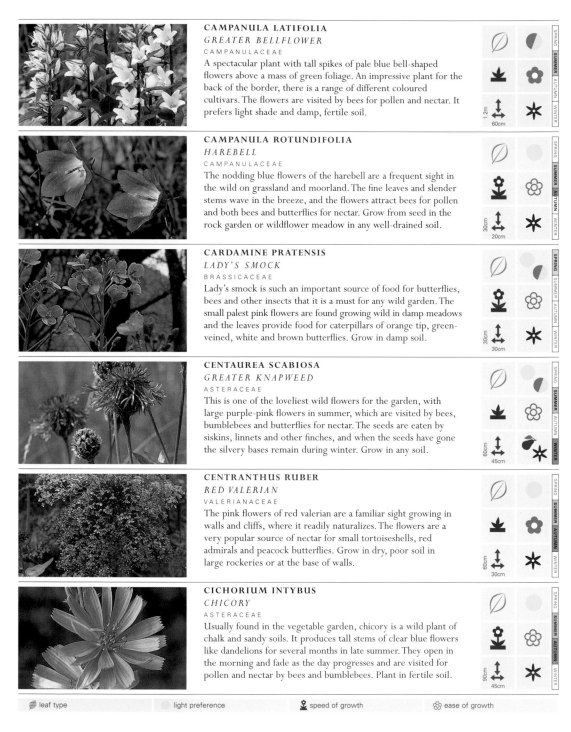

CAMPANULA LATIFOLIA
GREATER BELLFLOWER
CAMPANULACEAE

A spectacular plant with tall spikes of pale blue bell-shaped flowers above a mass of green foliage. An impressive plant for the back of the border, there is a range of different coloured cultivars. The flowers are visited by bees for pollen and nectar. It prefers light shade and damp, fertile soil.

1.2m / 60cm

CAMPANULA ROTUNDIFOLIA
HAREBELL
CAMPANULACEAE

The nodding blue flowers of the harebell are a frequent sight in the wild on grassland and moorland. The fine leaves and slender stems wave in the breeze, and the flowers attract bees for pollen and both bees and butterflies for nectar. Grow from seed in the rock garden or wildflower meadow in any well-drained soil.

30cm / 20cm

CARDAMINE PRATENSIS
LADY'S SMOCK
BRASSICACEAE

Lady's smock is such an important source of food for butterflies, bees and other insects that it is a must for any wild garden. The small palest pink flowers are found growing wild in damp meadows and the leaves provide food for caterpillars of orange tip, green-veined, white and brown butterflies. Grow in damp soil.

30cm / 30cm

CENTAUREA SCABIOSA
GREATER KNAPWEED
ASTERACEAE

This is one of the loveliest wild flowers for the garden, with large purple-pink flowers in summer, which are visited by bees, bumblebees and butterflies for nectar. The seeds are eaten by siskins, linnets and other finches, and when the seeds have gone the silvery bases remain during winter. Grow in any soil.

60cm / 45cm

CENTRANTHUS RUBER
RED VALERIAN
VALERIANACEAE

The pink flowers of red valerian are a familiar sight growing in walls and cliffs, where it readily naturalizes. The flowers are a very popular source of nectar for small tortoiseshells, red admirals and peacock butterflies. Grow in dry, poor soil in large rockeries or at the base of walls.

60cm / 30cm

CICHORIUM INTYBUS
CHICORY
ASTERACEAE

Usually found in the vegetable garden, chicory is a wild plant of chalk and sandy soils. It produces tall stems of clear blue flowers like dandelions for several months in late summer. They open in the morning and fade as the day progresses and are visited for pollen and nectar by bees and bumblebees. Plant in fertile soil.

90cm / 45cm

🌿 leaf type   ● light preference   ⚘ speed of growth   ⚙ ease of growth

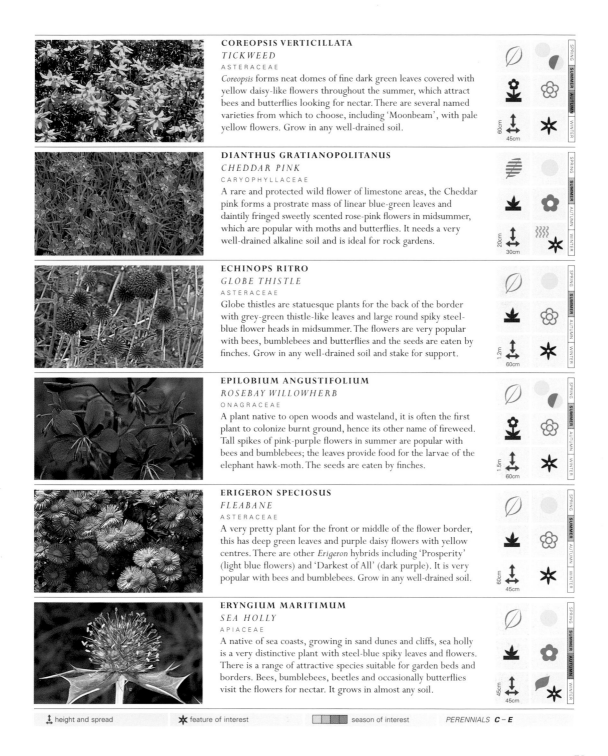

COREOPSIS VERTICILLATA
TICKWEED
ASTERACEAE

Coreopsis forms neat domes of fine dark green leaves covered with yellow daisy-like flowers throughout the summer, which attract bees and butterflies looking for nectar. There are several named varieties from which to choose, including 'Moonbeam', with pale yellow flowers. Grow in any well-drained soil.

60cm / 45cm

DIANTHUS GRATIANOPOLITANUS
CHEDDAR PINK
CARYOPHYLLACEAE

A rare and protected wild flower of limestone areas, the Cheddar pink forms a prostrate mass of linear blue-green leaves and daintily fringed sweetly scented rose-pink flowers in midsummer, which are popular with moths and butterflies. It needs a very well-drained alkaline soil and is ideal for rock gardens.

20cm / 30cm

ECHINOPS RITRO
GLOBE THISTLE
ASTERACEAE

Globe thistles are statuesque plants for the back of the border with grey-green thistle-like leaves and large round spiky steel-blue flower heads in midsummer. The flowers are very popular with bees, bumblebees and butterflies and the seeds are eaten by finches. Grow in any well-drained soil and stake for support.

1.2m / 60cm

EPILOBIUM ANGUSTIFOLIUM
ROSEBAY WILLOWHERB
ONAGRACEAE

A plant native to open woods and wasteland, it is often the first plant to colonize burnt ground, hence its other name of fireweed. Tall spikes of pink-purple flowers in summer are popular with bees and bumblebees; the leaves provide food for the larvae of the elephant hawk-moth. The seeds are eaten by finches.

1.5m / 60cm

ERIGERON SPECIOSUS
FLEABANE
ASTERACEAE

A very pretty plant for the front or middle of the flower border, this has deep green leaves and purple daisy flowers with yellow centres. There are other *Erigeron* hybrids including 'Prosperity' (light blue flowers) and 'Darkest of All' (dark purple). It is very popular with bees and bumblebees. Grow in any well-drained soil.

60cm / 45cm

ERYNGIUM MARITIMUM
SEA HOLLY
APIACEAE

A native of sea coasts, growing in sand dunes and cliffs, sea holly is a very distinctive plant with steel-blue spiky leaves and flowers. There is a range of attractive species suitable for garden beds and borders. Bees, bumblebees, beetles and occasionally butterflies visit the flowers for nectar. It grows in almost any soil.

45cm / 45cm

↕ height and spread   ✳ feature of interest   ▭ season of interest   *PERENNIALS* **C – E**

HERBACEOUS PERENNIALS

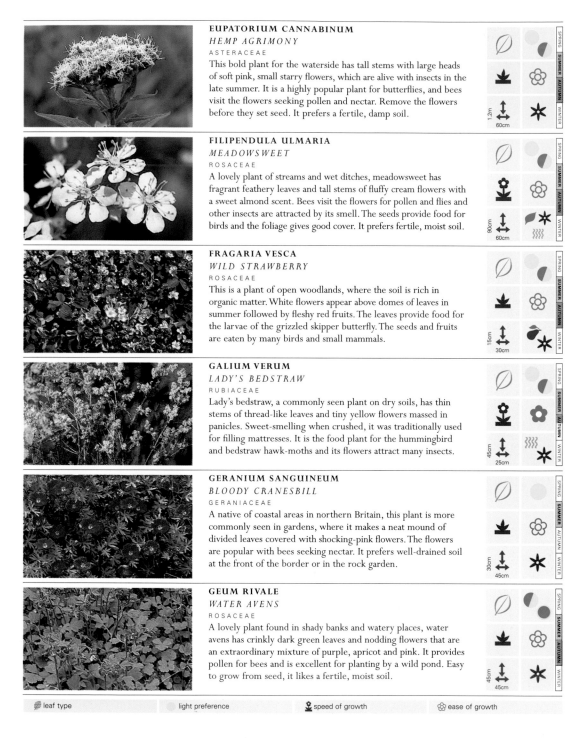

EUPATORIUM CANNABINUM
HEMP AGRIMONY
ASTERACEAE

This bold plant for the waterside has tall stems with large heads of soft pink, small starry flowers, which are alive with insects in the late summer. It is a highly popular plant for butterflies, and bees visit the flowers seeking pollen and nectar. Remove the flowers before they set seed. It prefers a fertile, damp soil.

1.2m / 60cm

FILIPENDULA ULMARIA
MEADOWSWEET
ROSACEAE

A lovely plant of streams and wet ditches, meadowsweet has fragrant feathery leaves and tall stems of fluffy cream flowers with a sweet almond scent. Bees visit the flowers for pollen and flies and other insects are attracted by its smell. The seeds provide food for birds and the foliage gives good cover. It prefers fertile, moist soil.

90cm / 60cm

FRAGARIA VESCA
WILD STRAWBERRY
ROSACEAE

This is a plant of open woodlands, where the soil is rich in organic matter. White flowers appear above domes of leaves in summer followed by fleshy red fruits. The leaves provide food for the larvae of the grizzled skipper butterfly. The seeds and fruits are eaten by many birds and small mammals.

15cm / 30cm

GALIUM VERUM
LADY'S BEDSTRAW
RUBIACEAE

Lady's bedstraw, a commonly seen plant on dry soils, has thin stems of thread-like leaves and tiny yellow flowers massed in panicles. Sweet-smelling when crushed, it was traditionally used for filling mattresses. It is the food plant for the hummingbird and bedstraw hawk-moths and its flowers attract many insects.

45cm / 25cm

GERANIUM SANGUINEUM
BLOODY CRANESBILL
GERANIACEAE

A native of coastal areas in northern Britain, this plant is more commonly seen in gardens, where it makes a neat mound of divided leaves covered with shocking-pink flowers. The flowers are popular with bees seeking nectar. It prefers well-drained soil at the front of the border or in the rock garden.

30cm / 45cm

GEUM RIVALE
WATER AVENS
ROSACEAE

A lovely plant found in shady banks and watery places, water avens has crinkly dark green leaves and nodding flowers that are an extraordinary mixture of purple, apricot and pink. It provides pollen for bees and is excellent for planting by a wild pond. Easy to grow from seed, it likes a fertile, moist soil.

45cm / 45cm

SPRING SUMMER AUTUMN WINTER

leaf type   light preference   speed of growth   ease of growth

HELIANTHEMUM NUMMULARIUM
ROCK ROSE

CISTACEAE

One of the best plants for covering a dry sunny bank, the rock rose has bright yellow flowers above prostrate stems of tiny green leaves. Many cultivated forms have flowers in almost every colour. The wild rock rose provides food for caterpillar larvae and the flowers provide pollen for bees.

HELLEBORUS FOETIDUS
STINKING HELLEBORE

RANUNCULACEAE

A native of old woodlands on chalky soils, this plant has dark green finger-like leaves and nodding green flowers edged with purple, which appear from midwinter and last into spring and even summer. The crushed leaves and seed pods give an idea as to the origin of its common name. The flowers provide early nectar for bees.

HESPERIS MATRONALIS
SWEET ROCKET

BRASSICACEAE

This widely naturalized plant has white or violet flowers that smell of violets during the day but have a clove-like scent in the evening. The flowers are a popular source of nectar for butterflies and the foliage is food for the orange-tip butterfly. Moths are attracted to the flowers. Grow in fertile, moist soil; allow to self-seed.

HIPPOCREPIS COMOSA
HORSESHOE VETCH

PAPILIONACEAE

A native of chalky hillsides, horseshoe vetch has delicate pinnate leaves and whorls of bright yellow pea flowers. It is the food plant for the larvae of dingy skipper, chalkhill blue and adonis blue butterflies, and the nectar is popular with both bees and butterflies. Grow in a wildflower meadow on well-drained soil.

HYPERICUM PERFORATUM
ST JOHN'S WORT

CLUSIACEAE

There are several species of St John's wort and this is the most adaptable and widespread, found in fields, hedgerows and woods. The leaves are fragrant and the starry yellow flowers have a sweet lemon scent. The seeds are eaten by blackcaps, bullfinches and redpolls. It can be invasive and the sap can cause skin allergies.

IRIS PSEUDACORUS
YELLOW FLAG

IRIDACEAE

A marvellous plant for any pond, the water iris will grow in water up to 15cm (6 in) deep or in damp borders. The tall sword-like leaves are used by dragonfly larvae as they emerge from the water and the yellow flowers provide nectar for bees and hoverflies. This is an essential plant for every wildlife pond.

⟂ height and spread   ✳ feature of interest   ▭ season of interest   *PERENNIALS* **E – I**

HERBACEOUS PERENNIALS

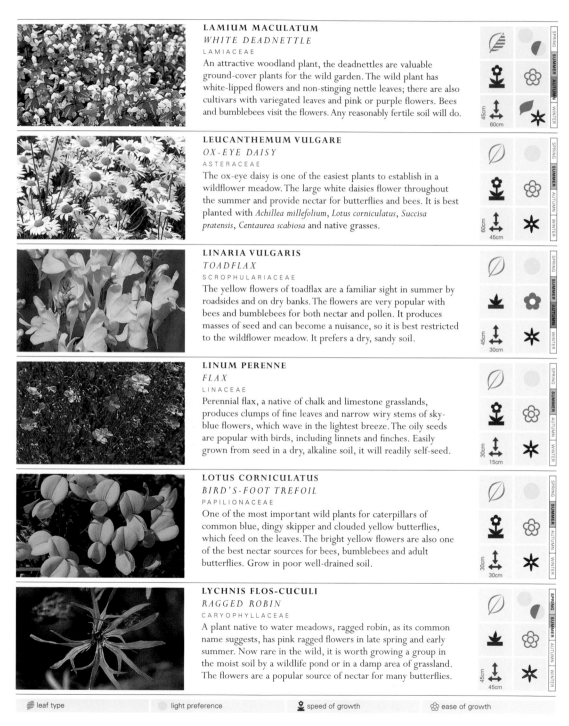

LAMIUM MACULATUM
WHITE DEADNETTLE
LAMIACEAE

An attractive woodland plant, the deadnettles are valuable ground-cover plants for the wild garden. The wild plant has white-lipped flowers and non-stinging nettle leaves; there are also cultivars with variegated leaves and pink or purple flowers. Bees and bumblebees visit the flowers. Any reasonably fertile soil will do.

LEUCANTHEMUM VULGARE
OX-EYE DAISY
ASTERACEAE

The ox-eye daisy is one of the easiest plants to establish in a wildflower meadow. The large white daisies flower throughout the summer and provide nectar for butterflies and bees. It is best planted with *Achillea millefolium*, *Lotus corniculatus*, *Succisa pratensis*, *Centaurea scabiosa* and native grasses.

LINARIA VULGARIS
TOADFLAX
SCROPHULARIACEAE

The yellow flowers of toadflax are a familiar sight in summer by roadsides and on dry banks. The flowers are very popular with bees and bumblebees for both nectar and pollen. It produces masses of seed and can become a nuisance, so it is best restricted to the wildflower meadow. It prefers a dry, sandy soil.

LINUM PERENNE
FLAX
LINACEAE

Perennial flax, a native of chalk and limestone grasslands, produces clumps of fine leaves and narrow wiry stems of sky-blue flowers, which wave in the lightest breeze. The oily seeds are popular with birds, including linnets and finches. Easily grown from seed in a dry, alkaline soil, it will readily self-seed.

LOTUS CORNICULATUS
BIRD'S-FOOT TREFOIL
PAPILIONACEAE

One of the most important wild plants for caterpillars of common blue, dingy skipper and clouded yellow butterflies, which feed on the leaves. The bright yellow flowers are also one of the best nectar sources for bees, bumblebees and adult butterflies. Grow in poor well-drained soil.

LYCHNIS FLOS-CUCULI
RAGGED ROBIN
CARYOPHYLLACEAE

A plant native to water meadows, ragged robin, as its common name suggests, has pink ragged flowers in late spring and early summer. Now rare in the wild, it is worth growing a group in the moist soil by a wildlife pond or in a damp area of grassland. The flowers are a popular source of nectar for many butterflies.

🌿 leaf type ● light preference 🌱 speed of growth ❀ ease of growth

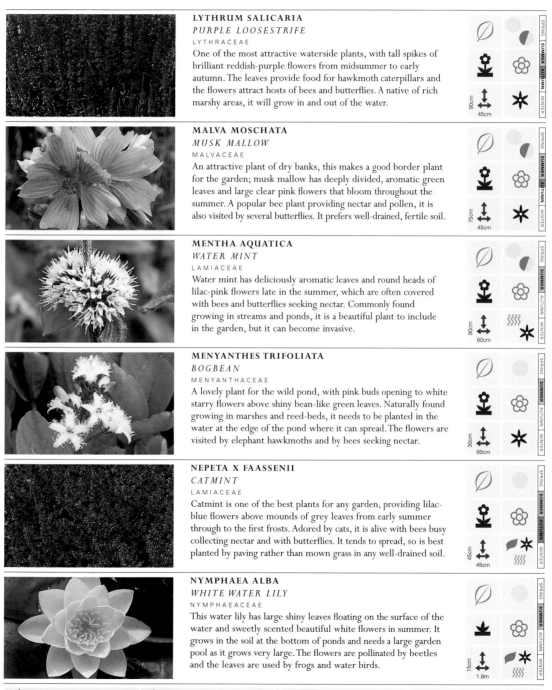

LYTHRUM SALICARIA
PURPLE LOOSESTRIFE
LYTHRACEAE

One of the most attractive waterside plants, with tall spikes of brilliant reddish-purple flowers from midsummer to early autumn. The leaves provide food for hawkmoth caterpillars and the flowers attract hosts of bees and butterflies. A native of rich marshy areas, it will grow in and out of the water.

90cm / 45cm

MALVA MOSCHATA
MUSK MALLOW
MALVACEAE

An attractive plant of dry banks, this makes a good border plant for the garden; musk mallow has deeply divided, aromatic green leaves and large clear pink flowers that bloom throughout the summer. A popular bee plant providing nectar and pollen, it is also visited by several butterflies. It prefers well-drained, fertile soil.

75cm / 45cm

MENTHA AQUATICA
WATER MINT
LAMIACEAE

Water mint has deliciously aromatic leaves and round heads of lilac-pink flowers late in the summer, which are often covered with bees and butterflies seeking nectar. Commonly found growing in streams and ponds, it is a beautiful plant to include in the garden, but it can become invasive.

90cm / 60cm

MENYANTHES TRIFOLIATA
BOGBEAN
MENYANTHACEAE

A lovely plant for the wild pond, with pink buds opening to white starry flowers above shiny bean-like green leaves. Naturally found growing in marshes and reed-beds, it needs to be planted in the water at the edge of the pond where it can spread. The flowers are visited by elephant hawkmoths and by bees seeking nectar.

30cm / 60cm

NEPETA X FAASSENII
CATMINT
LAMIACEAE

Catmint is one of the best plants for any garden, providing lilac-blue flowers above mounds of grey leaves from early summer through to the first frosts. Adored by cats, it is alive with bees busy collecting nectar and with butterflies. It tends to spread, so is best planted by paving rather than mown grass in any well-drained soil.

45cm / 45cm

NYMPHAEA ALBA
WHITE WATER LILY
NYMPHAEACEAE

This water lily has large shiny leaves floating on the surface of the water and sweetly scented beautiful white flowers in summer. It grows in the soil at the bottom of ponds and needs a large garden pool as it grows very large. The flowers are pollinated by beetles and the leaves are used by frogs and water birds.

15cm / 1.8m

⚓ height and spread   ✳ feature of interest   ▭ season of interest   *PERENNIALS* **L – N**

HERBACEOUS PERENNIALS

PARNASSIA PALUSTRIS
GRASS OF PARNASSUS
PARNASSIACEAE

A rare native of wet moorlands, this is a very pretty plant for the wild water garden. The heart-shaped dark green leaves give rise to upright stems of single-cupped, creamy-white flowers with green veining. The flowers are lightly scented and attract many insects. Plant in permanently wet, alkaline soil beside a pond.

PENSTEMON BARBATUS
SCROPHULARIACEAE

Penstemons are some of the very best flowers for gardens, with shiny leaves that stay green for most of the winter and spikes of glorious flowers produced through the summer and autumn right up until the first frosts occur. The flowers are very popular with both honeybees and bumblebees. Penstemons are easily grown in well-drained soil.

PERSICARIA BISTORTA
BISTORT
POLYGONACEAE

Bistort is a plant native to meadows and grass verges and one of the many attractive knotweeds that we can plant in our gardens. The poker-like spikes of pink flowers open throughout the summer and are frequently visited by bees and bumblebees, while birds feed on the seed heads in the autumn. Grow in well-drained soil.

PETASITES HYBRIDUS
BUTTERBUR
ASTERACEAE

A plant of streamsides and water meadows, butterbur has very large heart-shaped leaves and large heads of tiny pale lilac flowers in spring before the leaves appear. Early bees visit the flowers for nectar and pollen. Useful as ground cover in the damp soil around a pond, it needs space as it can become invasive.

PHLOX PANICULATA
POLEMONIACEAE

Phlox are one of the best flowering plants for the late summer border, with tall flat trusses of sweetly scented purple, white or pink flowers. The flowers are very popular with many butterflies and moths. There are many cultivars to choose from. They are at their best grown in rich moist soil in light shade but will grow in almost any garden conditions.

PLANTAGO MAJOR
GREAT PLANTAIN
PLANTAGINACEAE

Plantain is a familiar wild plant that occurs as a weed in lawns, with large ribbed leaves and wiry stems of small greenish flowers followed by capsules of small seeds. The leaves are the food plant for greater fritillary butterfly larvae and the seeds are eaten by several birds, including dunnocks. Grow in well-drained soil.

| leaf type | light preference | speed of growth | ease of growth |

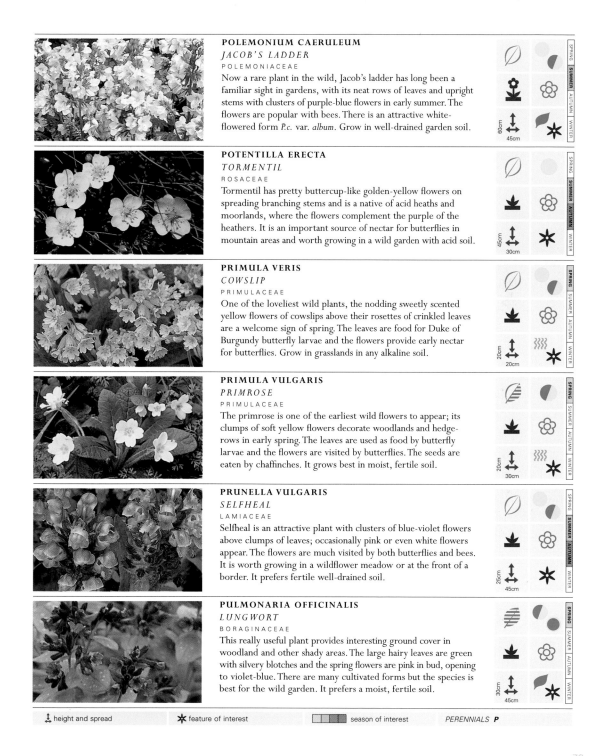

POLEMONIUM CAERULEUM
JACOB'S LADDER
POLEMONIACEAE
Now a rare plant in the wild, Jacob's ladder has long been a familiar sight in gardens, with its neat rows of leaves and upright stems with clusters of purple-blue flowers in early summer. The flowers are popular with bees. There is an attractive white-flowered form *P.c.* var. *album*. Grow in well-drained garden soil.

POTENTILLA ERECTA
TORMENTIL
ROSACEAE
Tormentil has pretty buttercup-like golden-yellow flowers on spreading branching stems and is a native of acid heaths and moorlands, where the flowers complement the purple of the heathers. It is an important source of nectar for butterflies in mountain areas and worth growing in a wild garden with acid soil.

PRIMULA VERIS
COWSLIP
PRIMULACEAE
One of the loveliest wild plants, the nodding sweetly scented yellow flowers of cowslips above their rosettes of crinkled leaves are a welcome sign of spring. The leaves are food for Duke of Burgundy butterfly larvae and the flowers provide early nectar for butterflies. Grow in grasslands in any alkaline soil.

PRIMULA VULGARIS
PRIMROSE
PRIMULACEAE
The primrose is one of the earliest wild flowers to appear; its clumps of soft yellow flowers decorate woodlands and hedge-rows in early spring. The leaves are used as food by butterfly larvae and the flowers are visited by butterflies. The seeds are eaten by chaffinches. It grows best in moist, fertile soil.

PRUNELLA VULGARIS
SELFHEAL
LAMIACEAE
Selfheal is an attractive plant with clusters of blue-violet flowers above clumps of leaves; occasionally pink or even white flowers appear. The flowers are much visited by both butterflies and bees. It is worth growing in a wildflower meadow or at the front of a border. It prefers fertile well-drained soil.

PULMONARIA OFFICINALIS
LUNGWORT
BORAGINACEAE
This really useful plant provides interesting ground cover in woodland and other shady areas. The large hairy leaves are green with silvery blotches and the spring flowers are pink in bud, opening to violet-blue. There are many cultivated forms but the species is best for the wild garden. It prefers a moist, fertile soil.

⚊ height and spread   ✳ feature of interest   season of interest   *PERENNIALS* **P**

HERBACEOUS PERENNIALS

PULSATILLA VULGARIS
PASQUEFLOWER
RANUNCULACEAE

A rare native of calcareous soils, this is an attractive plant for rock or herb gardens. The feathery silky leaves are very decorative and silky buds open to rich purple nodding flowers followed by silky seed heads. Visited by bees for pollen, the pasqueflower prefers a well-drained alkaline soil and is mildly poisonous.

20cm / 30cm

RANUNCULUS FICARIA
LESSER CELANDINE
RANUNCULACEAE

A native of damp shady places, this plant spreads rapidly in the right conditions. The dark green leaves form dense ground cover and shiny starry bright yellow flowers appear in early spring. They are popular with many insects, including bees and the grizzled skipper butterfly. Any moist soil is suitable.

10cm / 30cm

RUDBECKIA FULGIDA VAR. DEAMII
CONEFLOWER
ASTERACEAE

Coneflowers enhance our borders for most of the summer and autumn. The bright yellow daisy flowers have raised dark brown centres and are very popular with bees and bumblebees for nectar. This is one of the smaller forms, which does not need staking. Any reasonable garden soil is suitable.

60cm / 45cm

RUMEX CRISPUS
CURLED DOCK
POLYGONACEAE

Docks are best known for their use in easing nettle stings. Not usually grown in the garden, there should be room for a patch in a larger garden aiming to attract wildlife. The large shiny leaves are food for the larvae of the small copper butterfly and the seeds are eaten by reed buntings, jackdaws and finches.

90cm / 30cm

SAGITTARIA SAGITTIFOLIA
ARROW HEAD
ALISMATACEAE

One of the most dramatic of waterside plants, this has large arrow-shaped leaves and stiff flower stems with white papery blossoms with black centres in late summer. It prefers to grow in shallow water at the edge of the pond or in permanently wet mud. It is a good plant for ornamental or wild-garden pools.

60cm / 60cm

SANGUISORBA MINOR
SALAD BURNET
ROSACEAE

Salad burnet has pretty blue-green serrated leaves and small greenish-red pompom flower heads. The aromatic leaves have a cucumber-like flavour, and can be used in salads and sauces. It is good for planting in grass or in borders of well-drained or even dry soil; the flowers are occasionally visited by bees for pollen.

40cm / 30cm

SPRING | SUMMER | AUTUMN | WINTER

---

leaf type   light preference   speed of growth   ease of growth

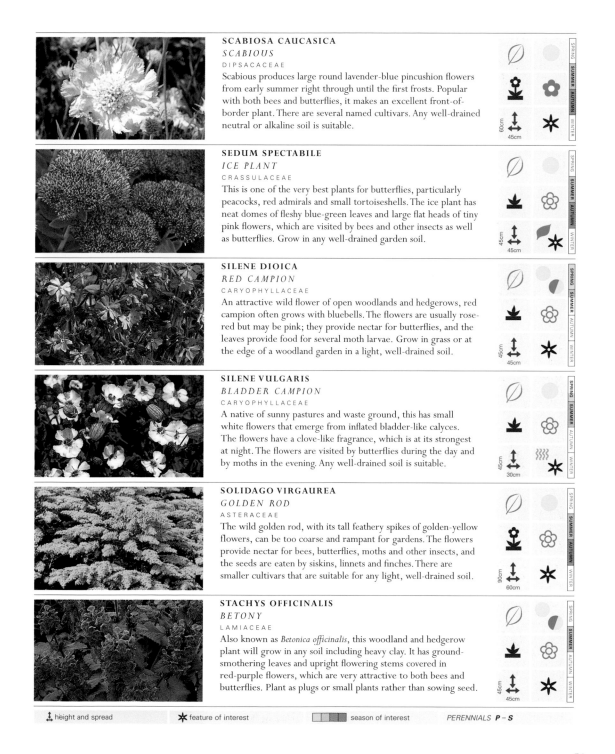

SCABIOSA CAUCASICA
SCABIOUS
DIPSACACEAE

Scabious produces large round lavender-blue pincushion flowers from early summer right through until the first frosts. Popular with both bees and butterflies, it makes an excellent front-of-border plant. There are several named cultivars. Any well-drained neutral or alkaline soil is suitable.

60cm / 45cm

SEDUM SPECTABILE
ICE PLANT
CRASSULACEAE

This is one of the very best plants for butterflies, particularly peacocks, red admirals and small tortoiseshells. The ice plant has neat domes of fleshy blue-green leaves and large flat heads of tiny pink flowers, which are visited by bees and other insects as well as butterflies. Grow in any well-drained garden soil.

45cm / 45cm

SILENE DIOICA
RED CAMPION
CARYOPHYLLACEAE

An attractive wild flower of open woodlands and hedgerows, red campion often grows with bluebells. The flowers are usually rose-red but may be pink; they provide nectar for butterflies, and the leaves provide food for several moth larvae. Grow in grass or at the edge of a woodland garden in a light, well-drained soil.

45cm / 45cm

SILENE VULGARIS
BLADDER CAMPION
CARYOPHYLLACEAE

A native of sunny pastures and waste ground, this has small white flowers that emerge from inflated bladder-like calyces. The flowers have a clove-like fragrance, which is at its strongest at night. The flowers are visited by butterflies during the day and by moths in the evening. Any well-drained soil is suitable.

45cm / 30cm

SOLIDAGO VIRGAUREA
GOLDEN ROD
ASTERACEAE

The wild golden rod, with its tall feathery spikes of golden-yellow flowers, can be too coarse and rampant for gardens. The flowers provide nectar for bees, butterflies, moths and other insects, and the seeds are eaten by siskins, linnets and finches. There are smaller cultivars that are suitable for any light, well-drained soil.

90cm / 60cm

STACHYS OFFICINALIS
BETONY
LAMIACEAE

Also known as *Betonica officinalis*, this woodland and hedgerow plant will grow in any soil including heavy clay. It has ground-smothering leaves and upright flowering stems covered in red-purple flowers, which are very attractive to both bees and butterflies. Plant as plugs or small plants rather than sowing seed.

45cm / 45cm

↕ height and spread   ✶ feature of interest   ▭▭▭ season of interest   *PERENNIALS* **P – S**

HERBACEOUS PERENNIALS

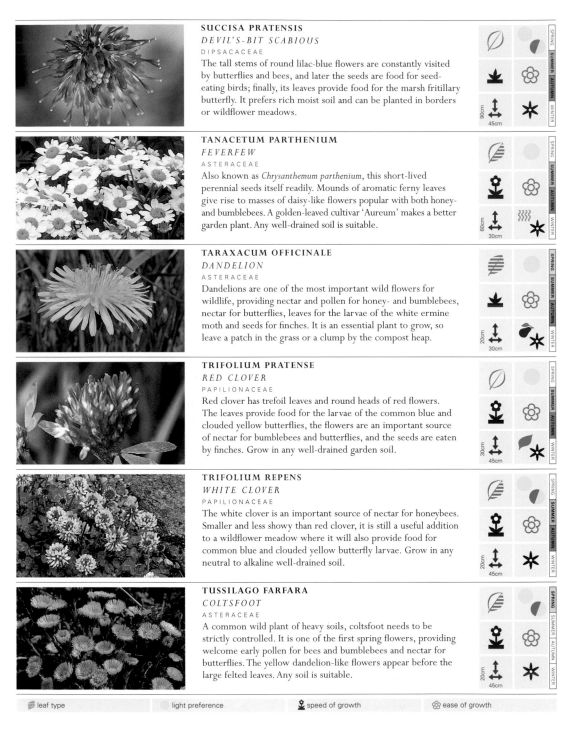

SUCCISA PRATENSIS
DEVIL'S-BIT SCABIOUS
DIPSACACEAE

The tall stems of round lilac-blue flowers are constantly visited by butterflies and bees, and later the seeds are food for seed-eating birds; finally, its leaves provide food for the marsh fritillary butterfly. It prefers rich moist soil and can be planted in borders or wildflower meadows.

TANACETUM PARTHENIUM
FEVERFEW
ASTERACEAE

Also known as *Chrysanthemum parthenium*, this short-lived perennial seeds itself readily. Mounds of aromatic ferny leaves give rise to masses of daisy-like flowers popular with both honey- and bumblebees. A golden-leaved cultivar 'Aureum' makes a better garden plant. Any well-drained soil is suitable.

TARAXACUM OFFICINALE
DANDELION
ASTERACEAE

Dandelions are one of the most important wild flowers for wildlife, providing nectar and pollen for honey- and bumblebees, nectar for butterflies, leaves for the larvae of the white ermine moth and seeds for finches. It is an essential plant to grow, so leave a patch in the grass or a clump by the compost heap.

TRIFOLIUM PRATENSE
RED CLOVER
PAPILIONACEAE

Red clover has trefoil leaves and round heads of red flowers. The leaves provide food for the larvae of the common blue and clouded yellow butterflies, the flowers are an important source of nectar for bumblebees and butterflies, and the seeds are eaten by finches. Grow in any well-drained garden soil.

TRIFOLIUM REPENS
WHITE CLOVER
PAPILIONACEAE

The white clover is an important source of nectar for honeybees. Smaller and less showy than red clover, it is still a useful addition to a wildflower meadow where it will also provide food for common blue and clouded yellow butterfly larvae. Grow in any neutral to alkaline well-drained soil.

TUSSILAGO FARFARA
COLTSFOOT
ASTERACEAE

A common wild plant of heavy soils, coltsfoot needs to be strictly controlled. It is one of the first spring flowers, providing welcome early pollen for bees and bumblebees and nectar for butterflies. The yellow dandelion-like flowers appear before the large felted leaves. Any soil is suitable.

≣ leaf type	light preference	⚘ speed of growth	⊕ ease of growth

URTICA DIOICA
STINGING NETTLE
URTICACEAE
Every wildlife garden needs a patch of stinging nettles to provide food for the caterpillars of many of the aristocrat butterflies. The caterpillars will then provide food for many garden birds, and finches will enjoy the nettle seeds. Plant a nettle bed in fertile soil in a a sheltered corner of the garden.

1.2m / 60cm

VALERIANA OFFICINALIS
VALERIAN
VALERIANACEAE
A native of marshes and boggy areas, valerian is a very adaptable plant for the garden either planted by ponds or in beds and borders. It has tall stems with clusters of small pink flowers, which provide nectar for many butterflies. Cats also love the plant. Almost any soil is fine, although it prefers damp conditions.

90cm / 30cm

VERBASCUM NIGRUM
DARK MULLEIN
SCROPHULARIACEAE
This makes a good border plant with its large dark green leaves, with downy under-sides, and its tall narrow spikes of purple-centred yellow flowers in summer and early autumn. Bees visit the flowers for pollen and butterflies for nectar. It seeds itself freely and prefers well-drained, chalky soil.

1.2m / 45cm

VERONICA SPICATA
SPIKED SPEEDWELL
SCROPHULARIACEAE
This speedwell, although quite rare in the wild, is found in many gardens, where its neat domes of green leaves give rise to slender spikes of bright blue flowers in early summer. These are very popular with bees, who seek out the flowers for both pollen and nectar. It is a good border plant for well-drained soil.

60cm / 45cm

VIOLA ODORATA
SWEET VIOLET
VIOLACEAE
The sweet violet has scented deep purple flowers above domes of heart-shaped leaves, which carpet our woods in early spring. The leaves provide food for the larvae of many of the fritillary butterflies and the seeds are eaten by coal tits, bullfinches and woodpipers. It prefers a humus-rich, moist soil.

10cm / 30cm

VIOLA RIVINIANA
COMMON DOG VIOLET
VIOLACEAE
This is a smaller-flowered violet than *Viola odorata*. A plant of woodlands, it is often seen growing with primroses at the base of hedges. The leaves are the major food plant for the larvae of many fritillary butterflies and the adults visit the plants to lay their eggs. It prefers a moist, humus-rich soil.

10cm / 30cm

⭥ height and spread   ✳ feature of interest   ▭▭▭▭ season of interest   *PERENNIALS **S – V***

GRASSES AND FERNS

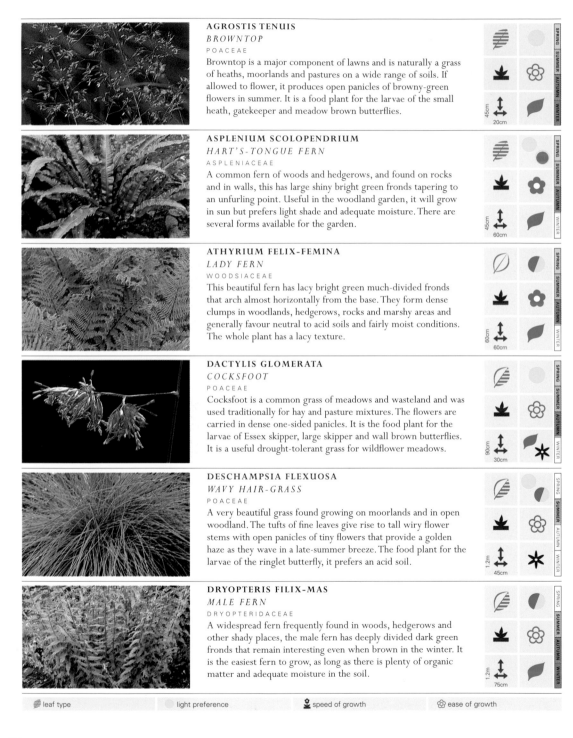

AGROSTIS TENUIS
BROWNTOP
POACEAE

Browntop is a major component of lawns and is naturally a grass of heaths, moorlands and pastures on a wide range of soils. If allowed to flower, it produces open panicles of browny-green flowers in summer. It is a food plant for the larvae of the small heath, gatekeeper and meadow brown butterflies.

ASPLENIUM SCOLOPENDRIUM
HART'S-TONGUE FERN
ASPLENIACEAE

A common fern of woods and hedgerows, and found on rocks and in walls, this has large shiny bright green fronds tapering to an unfurling point. Useful in the woodland garden, it will grow in sun but prefers light shade and adequate moisture. There are several forms available for the garden.

ATHYRIUM FELIX-FEMINA
LADY FERN
WOODSIACEAE

This beautiful fern has lacy bright green much-divided fronds that arch almost horizontally from the base. They form dense clumps in woodlands, hedgerows, rocks and marshy areas and generally favour neutral to acid soils and fairly moist conditions. The whole plant has a lacy texture.

DACTYLIS GLOMERATA
COCKSFOOT
POACEAE

Cocksfoot is a common grass of meadows and wasteland and was used traditionally for hay and pasture mixtures. The flowers are carried in dense one-sided panicles. It is the food plant for the larvae of Essex skipper, large skipper and wall brown butterflies. It is a useful drought-tolerant grass for wildflower meadows.

DESCHAMPSIA FLEXUOSA
WAVY HAIR-GRASS
POACEAE

A very beautiful grass found growing on moorlands and in open woodland. The tufts of fine leaves give rise to tall wiry flower stems with open panicles of tiny flowers that provide a golden haze as they wave in a late-summer breeze. The food plant for the larvae of the ringlet butterfly, it prefers an acid soil.

DRYOPTERIS FILIX-MAS
MALE FERN
DRYOPTERIDACEAE

A widespread fern frequently found in woods, hedgerows and other shady places, the male fern has deeply divided dark green fronds that remain interesting even when brown in the winter. It is the easiest fern to grow, as long as there is plenty of organic matter and adequate moisture in the soil.

leaf type | light preference | speed of growth | ease of growth

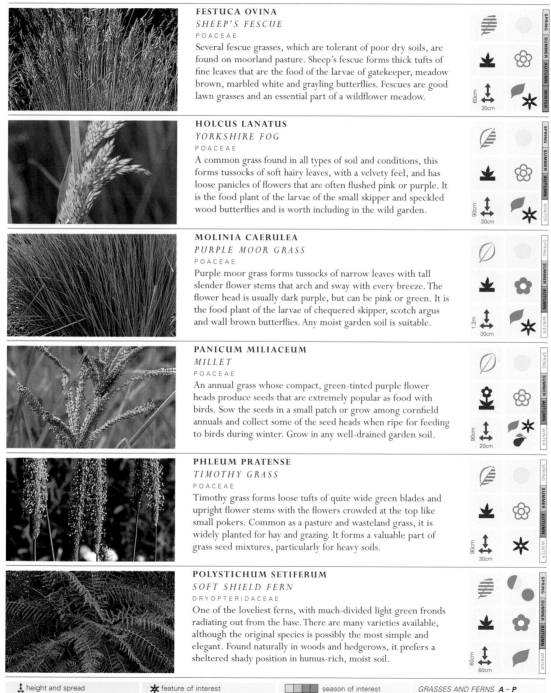

FESTUCA OVINA
SHEEP'S FESCUE
POACEAE

Several fescue grasses, which are tolerant of poor dry soils, are found on moorland pasture. Sheep's fescue forms thick tufts of fine leaves that are the food of the larvae of gatekeeper, meadow brown, marbled white and grayling butterflies. Fescues are good lawn grasses and an essential part of a wildflower meadow.

60cm / 30cm

HOLCUS LANATUS
YORKSHIRE FOG
POACEAE

A common grass found in all types of soil and conditions, this forms tussocks of soft hairy leaves, with a velvety feel, and has loose panicles of flowers that are often flushed pink or purple. It is the food plant of the larvae of the small skipper and speckled wood butterflies and is worth including in the wild garden.

90cm / 30cm

MOLINIA CAERULEA
PURPLE MOOR GRASS
POACEAE

Purple moor grass forms tussocks of narrow leaves with tall slender flower stems that arch and sway with every breeze. The flower head is usually dark purple, but can be pink or green. It is the food plant of the larvae of chequered skipper, scotch argus and wall brown butterflies. Any moist garden soil is suitable.

1.2m / 30cm

PANICUM MILIACEUM
MILLET
POACEAE

An annual grass whose compact, green-tinted purple flower heads produce seeds that are extremely popular as food with birds. Sow the seeds in a small patch or grow among cornfield annuals and collect some of the seed heads when ripe for feeding to birds during winter. Grow in any well-drained garden soil.

90cm / 20cm

PHLEUM PRATENSE
TIMOTHY GRASS
POACEAE

Timothy grass forms loose tufts of quite wide green blades and upright flower stems with the flowers crowded at the top like small pokers. Common as a pasture and wasteland grass, it is widely planted for hay and grazing. It forms a valuable part of grass seed mixtures, particularly for heavy soils.

90cm / 30cm

POLYSTICHUM SETIFERUM
SOFT SHIELD FERN
DRYOPTERIDACEAE

One of the loveliest ferns, with much-divided light green fronds radiating out from the base. There are many varieties available, although the original species is possibly the most simple and elegant. Found naturally in woods and hedgerows, it prefers a sheltered shady position in humus-rich, moist soil.

60cm / 60cm

SPRING | SUMMER | AUTUMN | WINTER

⬍ height and spread   ✳ feature of interest   ▭ season of interest   *GRASSES AND FERNS* **A – P**

SHRUBS

ARALIA ELATA
JAPANESE ANGELICA TREE
ARALIACEAE

An architectural shrub with very large elegant grey-green leaves, and upright open trusses of white flowers in late summer that are sweetly scented and attract bees looking for nectar. There are also cultivars with variegated leaves. It prefers fertile well-drained neutral soils.

BERBERIS THUNBERGII
BARBERRY
BERBERIDACEAE

There are dozens of different barberries, and this is one of the most popular, with many cultivars with coloured leaves and a range of shapes and sizes. The small hanging flowers are visited by bees and bumblebees in spring and the red glossy fruits are food for birds in autumn. Any soil is suitable.

BUDDLEJA DAVIDII
BUTTERFLY BUSH
BUDDLEJACEAE

Buddleja is a major source of nectar for butterflies, including red admiral, comma, small tortoiseshell, peacock and painted lady. It is a large shrub with grey-green leaves and cones of scented lilac flowers in summer and autumn, which are also attractive to bees and bumblebees. It tolerates a wide range of soils and conditions.

BUDDLEJA GLOBOSA
BUDDLEJACEAE

This *Buddleja* has dark green leaves with silver undersides that remain through a mild winter and globes of bright yellow-orange flowers with a strong sweet honey scent. It appears to attract more bees than the *B. davidii*, but not quite so many butterflies. It prefers a sheltered sunny spot with a rich deep soil but is tolerant of most conditions.

BUXUS SEMPERVIRENS
BOX
BUXACEAE

Box makes a useful garden plant, whether left unclipped to flower or clipped into ornamental topiary or hedges. Round dark green aromatic leaves cover the branches and fluffy yellow flowers appear on older plants and attract bees for nectar and pollen. It is tolerant of most soils, but prefers a rich, fertile one.

CALLUNA VULGARIS
LING
ERICACEAE

This heather covers moorlands with a purple haze of flowers. The wiry stems carry tiny leaves and spikes of purple-pink flowers, an important source of nectar for honeybees. It is also the food plant for the larvae of the silver-studded blue butterfly and the emperor moth, and birds eat the seeds. Acid soil is essential.

≡ leaf type   ● light preference   ♣ speed of growth   ✤ ease of growth

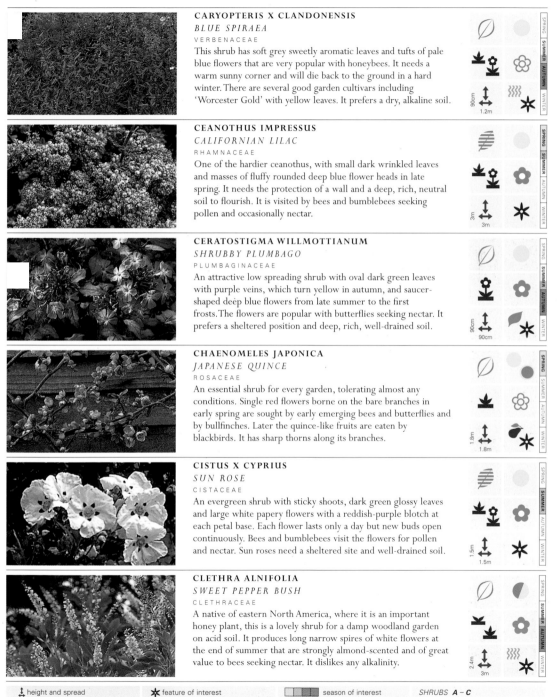

CARYOPTERIS X CLANDONENSIS
BLUE SPIRAEA
VERBENACEAE

This shrub has soft grey sweetly aromatic leaves and tufts of pale blue flowers that are very popular with honeybees. It needs a warm sunny corner and will die back to the ground in a hard winter. There are several good garden cultivars including 'Worcester Gold' with yellow leaves. It prefers a dry, alkaline soil.

CEANOTHUS IMPRESSUS
CALIFORNIAN LILAC
RHAMNACEAE

One of the hardier ceanothus, with small dark wrinkled leaves and masses of fluffy rounded deep blue flower heads in late spring. It needs the protection of a wall and a deep, rich, neutral soil to flourish. It is visited by bees and bumblebees seeking pollen and occasionally nectar.

CERATOSTIGMA WILLMOTTIANUM
SHRUBBY PLUMBAGO
PLUMBAGINACEAE

An attractive low spreading shrub with oval dark green leaves with purple veins, which turn yellow in autumn, and saucer-shaped deep blue flowers from late summer to the first frosts. The flowers are popular with butterflies seeking nectar. It prefers a sheltered position and deep, rich, well-drained soil.

CHAENOMELES JAPONICA
JAPANESE QUINCE
ROSACEAE

An essential shrub for every garden, tolerating almost any conditions. Single red flowers borne on the bare branches in early spring are sought by early emerging bees and butterflies and by bullfinches. Later the quince-like fruits are eaten by blackbirds. It has sharp thorns along its branches.

CISTUS X CYPRIUS
SUN ROSE
CISTACEAE

An evergreen shrub with sticky shoots, dark green glossy leaves and large white papery flowers with a reddish-purple blotch at each petal base. Each flower lasts only a day but new buds open continuously. Bees and bumblebees visit the flowers for pollen and nectar. Sun roses need a sheltered site and well-drained soil.

CLETHRA ALNIFOLIA
SWEET PEPPER BUSH
CLETHRACEAE

A native of eastern North America, where it is an important honey plant, this is a lovely shrub for a damp woodland garden on acid soil. It produces long narrow spires of white flowers at the end of summer that are strongly almond-scented and of great value to bees seeking nectar. It dislikes any alkalinity.

↕ height and spread   ✳ feature of interest   ▭▭▭▭ season of interest   *SHRUBS* **A – C**

SHRUBS

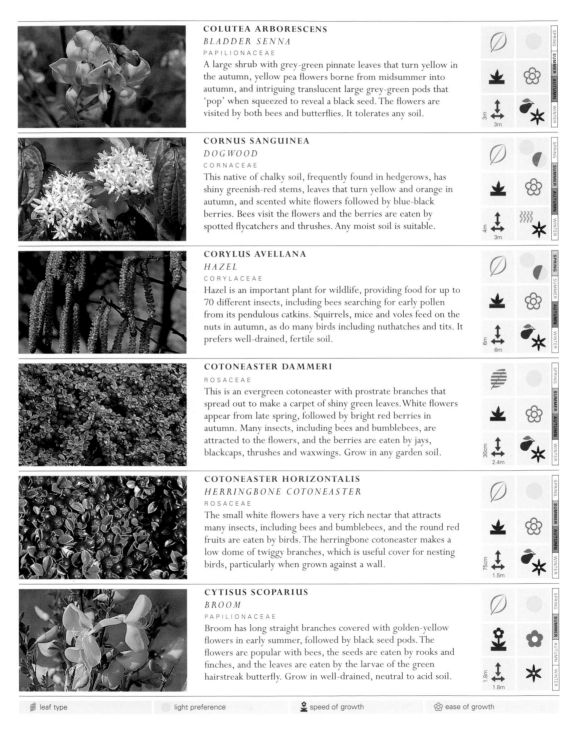

COLUTEA ARBORESCENS
BLADDER SENNA
PAPILIONACEAE

A large shrub with grey-green pinnate leaves that turn yellow in the autumn, yellow pea flowers borne from midsummer into autumn, and intriguing translucent large grey-green pods that 'pop' when squeezed to reveal a black seed. The flowers are visited by both bees and butterflies. It tolerates any soil.

CORNUS SANGUINEA
DOGWOOD
CORNACEAE

This native of chalky soil, frequently found in hedgerows, has shiny greenish-red stems, leaves that turn yellow and orange in autumn, and scented white flowers followed by blue-black berries. Bees visit the flowers and the berries are eaten by spotted flycatchers and thrushes. Any moist soil is suitable.

CORYLUS AVELLANA
HAZEL
CORYLACEAE

Hazel is an important plant for wildlife, providing food for up to 70 different insects, including bees searching for early pollen from its pendulous catkins. Squirrels, mice and voles feed on the nuts in autumn, as do many birds including nuthatches and tits. It prefers well-drained, fertile soil.

COTONEASTER DAMMERI
ROSACEAE

This is an evergreen cotoneaster with prostrate branches that spread out to make a carpet of shiny green leaves. White flowers appear from late spring, followed by bright red berries in autumn. Many insects, including bees and bumblebees, are attracted to the flowers, and the berries are eaten by jays, blackcaps, thrushes and waxwings. Grow in any garden soil.

COTONEASTER HORIZONTALIS
HERRINGBONE COTONEASTER
ROSACEAE

The small white flowers have a very rich nectar that attracts many insects, including bees and bumblebees, and the round red fruits are eaten by birds. The herringbone cotoneaster makes a low dome of twiggy branches, which is useful cover for nesting birds, particularly when grown against a wall.

CYTISUS SCOPARIUS
BROOM
PAPILIONACEAE

Broom has long straight branches covered with golden-yellow flowers in early summer, followed by black seed pods. The flowers are popular with bees, the seeds are eaten by rooks and finches, and the leaves are eaten by the larvae of the green hairstreak butterfly. Grow in well-drained, neutral to acid soil.

🍃 leaf type	🔵 light preference	♇ speed of growth	⚙ ease of growth

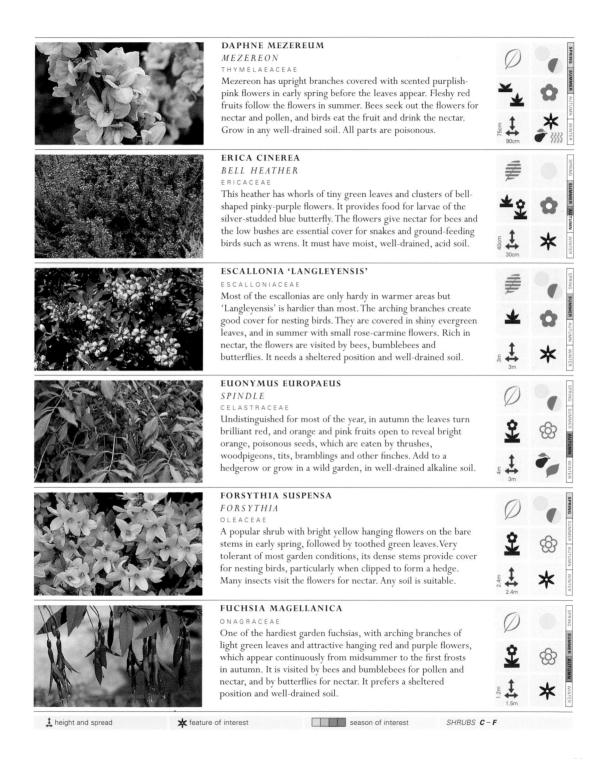

DAPHNE MEZEREUM
MEZEREON
THYMELAEACEAE

Mezereon has upright branches covered with scented purplish-pink flowers in early spring before the leaves appear. Fleshy red fruits follow the flowers in summer. Bees seek out the flowers for nectar and pollen, and birds eat the fruit and drink the nectar. Grow in any well-drained soil. All parts are poisonous.

ERICA CINEREA
BELL HEATHER
ERICACEAE

This heather has whorls of tiny green leaves and clusters of bell-shaped pinky-purple flowers. It provides food for larvae of the silver-studded blue butterfly. The flowers give nectar for bees and the low bushes are essential cover for snakes and ground-feeding birds such as wrens. It must have moist, well-drained, acid soil.

ESCALLONIA 'LANGLEYENSIS'
ESCALLONIACEAE

Most of the escallonias are only hardy in warmer areas but 'Langleyensis' is hardier than most. The arching branches create good cover for nesting birds. They are covered in shiny evergreen leaves, and in summer with small rose-carmine flowers. Rich in nectar, the flowers are visited by bees, bumblebees and butterflies. It needs a sheltered position and well-drained soil.

EUONYMUS EUROPAEUS
SPINDLE
CELASTRACEAE

Undistinguished for most of the year, in autumn the leaves turn brilliant red, and orange and pink fruits open to reveal bright orange, poisonous seeds, which are eaten by thrushes, woodpigeons, tits, bramblings and other finches. Add to a hedgerow or grow in a wild garden, in well-drained alkaline soil.

FORSYTHIA SUSPENSA
FORSYTHIA
OLEACEAE

A popular shrub with bright yellow hanging flowers on the bare stems in early spring, followed by toothed green leaves. Very tolerant of most garden conditions, its dense stems provide cover for nesting birds, particularly when clipped to form a hedge. Many insects visit the flowers for nectar. Any soil is suitable.

FUCHSIA MAGELLANICA
ONAGRACEAE

One of the hardiest garden fuchsias, with arching branches of light green leaves and attractive hanging red and purple flowers, which appear continuously from midsummer to the first frosts in autumn. It is visited by bees and bumblebees for pollen and nectar, and by butterflies for nectar. It prefers a sheltered position and well-drained soil.

⤢ height and spread   ✳ feature of interest   ▭▭ season of interest   *SHRUBS* **C – F**

SHRUBS

HEBE SALICIFOLIA
SHRUBBY VERONICA
SCROPHULARIACEAE

This is one of the best and hardiest hebes with long shiny bright green leaves and pale lilac flowers in short spikes through summer and into autumn. Both bees and bumblebees visit the flowers for nectar, as do many butterflies including red admirals and small tortoiseshells. Any well-drained soil is suitable.

2.4m
2.4m

HIPPOPHAE RHAMNOIDES
SEA BUCKTHORN
ELAEAGNACEAE

Found on coastal sand dunes, the sea buckthorn has spiny branches with attractive silvery-grey leaves that turn yellow in autumn. The inconspicuous flowers are followed by round orange berries on the female plants. The flowers are visited by bumblebees and the fruits taken by birds. Grow in a light soil.

6m
6m

HYDRANGEA QUERCIFOLIA
OAK LEAF HYDRANGEA
HYDRANGEACEAE

The oak leaf hydrangea has attractive lobed leaves and panicles of white flowers that stay on the plant into autumn. Bees visit the flowers for pollen and nectar, and butterflies also come for nectar. Best grown in fertile well-drained soil in sun to attract insects, it will, however, tolerate deep shade.

2.1m
2.1m

ILEX AQUIFOLIUM
HOLLY
AQUIFOLIACEAE

An excellent wildlife plant with prickly dark green leaves, clusters of white flowers in spring and bright red berries in autumn and winter. Honeybees source nectar from the flowers, birds eat the berries, the larvae of the holly blue butterfly eat the flower buds, and birds nest in its branches. Any soil is suitable.

6m
4m

JUNIPERUS COMMUNIS
JUNIPER
CUPRESSACEAE

Juniper is found chiefly on limestone and chalk soils. The usually rather low bushes are covered in tightly packed needles which make good safe cover for nesting birds. The cone is a black fleshy fruit which is eaten by treecreepers, thrushes and finches. Any well-drained soil is suitable.

6m
4m

LAVATERA ARBOREA
TREE MALLOW
MALVACEAE

The tree mallow has crinkled downy leaves and large pinkish-purple papery flowers in summer with wide open centres that attract bees, butterflies and other insects seeking nectar. There are several attractive garden forms which are equally good. It prefers a poor, well-drained soil and shelter from cold winds.

1.5m
4m

leaf type	light preference	speed of growth	ease of growth

LIGUSTRUM OVALIFOLIUM
OVAL-LEAVED PRIVET
OLEACEAE

A tall-growing evergreen with large shiny leaves. Available with variegated or gold leaves. All have open upright panicles of honey-scented creamy flowers that attract bees, butterflies and other insects, followed by dull black poisonous berries which are eaten by birds. Any fertile soil is suitable.

4m / 4m

LIGUSTRUM VULGARE
PRIVET
OLEACEAE

Privet has dull green leaves and clusters of creamy scented flowers in summer, followed by black shiny berries. It is the food plant for the privet hawk-moth and a source of nectar for bees, bumblebees and butterflies. Birds eat the poisonous fruit. It prefers a well-drained, alkaline soil.

6m / 3m

LONICERA X PURPUSII
WINTER HONEYSUCKLE
CAPRIFOLIACEAE

A lovely winter-flowering shrub with tangled branches of dark green leaves and small sweetly scented creamy-white flowers from late autumn throughout the winter. The flowers provide an early source of pollen for bees emerging from hibernation, and the branches create winter cover for birds. Grow in any soil.

1.8m / 1.8m

MAHONIA AQUIFOLIUM
OREGON GRAPE
BERBERIDACEAE

A spreading evergreen with dense glossy holly-like leaves, delicately scented bright yellow flowers in spring and blue-black fruits in autumn. Bees visit the flowers for nectar, as do house sparrows and blue tits, and the berries are eaten by blackbirds and mistle thrushes. Grow in any soil that is not too dry.

90cm / 1.5m

PEROVSKIA ATRIPLICIFOLIA
RUSSIAN SAGE
LAMIACEAE

An attractive shrub with aromatic grey-green serrated leaves and open spikes of small lavender-blue flowers in summer to autumn. The stems die back in winter but shoot strongly from the ground in spring. The flowers are popular with bees collecting nectar. It prefers a well-drained open soil.

1.5m / 60cm

POTENTILLA FRUTICOSA
SHRUBBY CINQUEFOIL
ROSACEAE

Potentilla forms a neat bush of tiny leaves, which is covered in small yellow saucer-shaped flowers throughout the summer. There are cultivars available in many different colours; all are popular with bees, bumblebees and butterflies seeking nectar. It prefers a sunny site and well-drained soil.

1.2m / 1.2m

SPRING SUMMER AUTUMN WINTER

⬍ height and spread   ✳ feature of interest   ▭ season of interest   *SHRUBS* **H – P**

SHRUBS

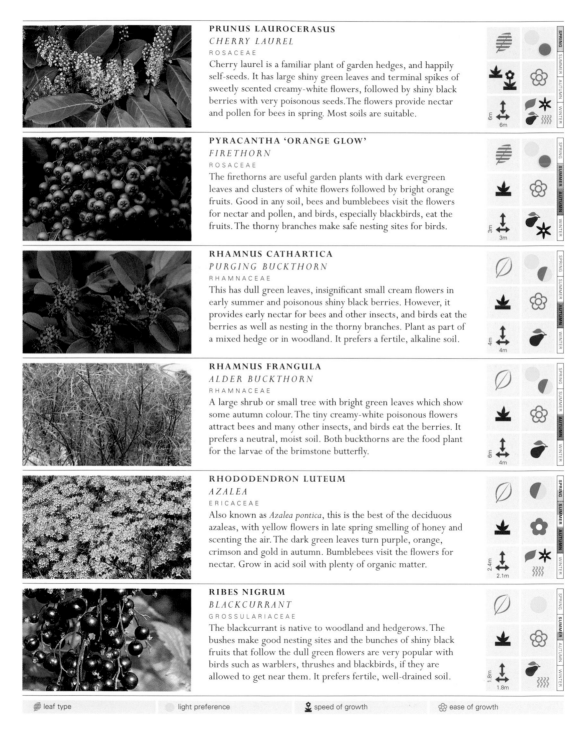

PRUNUS LAUROCERASUS
CHERRY LAUREL
ROSACEAE
Cherry laurel is a familiar plant of garden hedges, and happily self-seeds. It has large shiny green leaves and terminal spikes of sweetly scented creamy-white flowers, followed by shiny black berries with very poisonous seeds. The flowers provide nectar and pollen for bees in spring. Most soils are suitable.

PYRACANTHA 'ORANGE GLOW'
FIRETHORN
ROSACEAE
The firethorns are useful garden plants with dark evergreen leaves and clusters of white flowers followed by bright orange fruits. Good in any soil, bees and bumblebees visit the flowers for nectar and pollen, and birds, especially blackbirds, eat the fruits. The thorny branches make safe nesting sites for birds.

RHAMNUS CATHARTICA
PURGING BUCKTHORN
RHAMNACEAE
This has dull green leaves, insignificant small cream flowers in early summer and poisonous shiny black berries. However, it provides early nectar for bees and other insects, and birds eat the berries as well as nesting in the thorny branches. Plant as part of a mixed hedge or in woodland. It prefers a fertile, alkaline soil.

RHAMNUS FRANGULA
ALDER BUCKTHORN
RHAMNACEAE
A large shrub or small tree with bright green leaves which show some autumn colour. The tiny creamy-white poisonous flowers attract bees and many other insects, and birds eat the berries. It prefers a neutral, moist soil. Both buckthorns are the food plant for the larvae of the brimstone butterfly.

RHODODENDRON LUTEUM
AZALEA
ERICACEAE
Also known as *Azalea pontica*, this is the best of the deciduous azaleas, with yellow flowers in late spring smelling of honey and scenting the air. The dark green leaves turn purple, orange, crimson and gold in autumn. Bumblebees visit the flowers for nectar. Grow in acid soil with plenty of organic matter.

RIBES NIGRUM
BLACKCURRANT
GROSSULARIACEAE
The blackcurrant is native to woodland and hedgerows. The bushes make good nesting sites and the bunches of shiny black fruits that follow the dull green flowers are very popular with birds such as warblers, thrushes and blackbirds, if they are allowed to get near them. It prefers fertile, well-drained soil.

leaf type   light preference   speed of growth   ease of growth

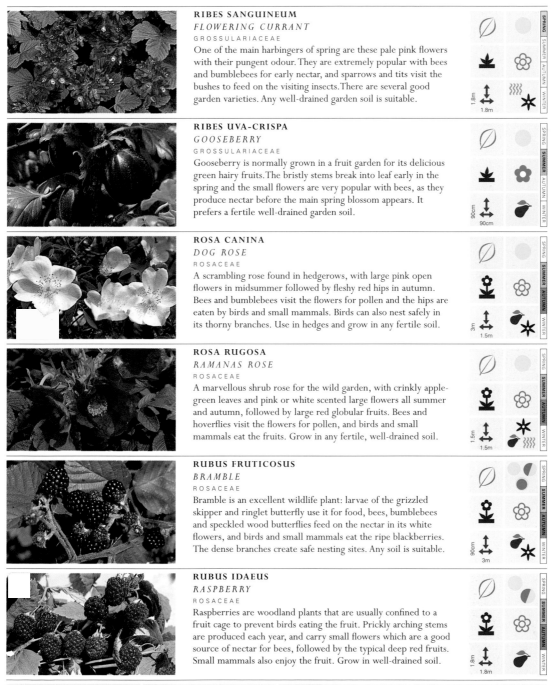

RIBES SANGUINEUM
FLOWERING CURRANT
GROSSULARIACEAE

One of the main harbingers of spring are these pale pink flowers with their pungent odour. They are extremely popular with bees and bumblebees for early nectar, and sparrows and tits visit the bushes to feed on the visiting insects. There are several good garden varieties. Any well-drained garden soil is suitable.

1.8m / 1.8m

SPRING SUMMER AUTUMN WINTER

RIBES UVA-CRISPA
GOOSEBERRY
GROSSULARIACEAE

Gooseberry is normally grown in a fruit garden for its delicious green hairy fruits. The bristly stems break into leaf early in the spring and the small flowers are very popular with bees, as they produce nectar before the main spring blossom appears. It prefers a fertile well-drained garden soil.

90cm / 90cm

SPRING SUMMER AUTUMN WINTER

ROSA CANINA
DOG ROSE
ROSACEAE

A scrambling rose found in hedgerows, with large pink open flowers in midsummer followed by fleshy red hips in autumn. Bees and bumblebees visit the flowers for pollen and the hips are eaten by birds and small mammals. Birds can also nest safely in its thorny branches. Use in hedges and grow in any fertile soil.

3m / 1.5m

SPRING SUMMER AUTUMN WINTER

ROSA RUGOSA
RAMANAS ROSE
ROSACEAE

A marvellous shrub rose for the wild garden, with crinkly apple-green leaves and pink or white scented large flowers all summer and autumn, followed by large red globular fruits. Bees and hoverflies visit the flowers for pollen, and birds and small mammals eat the fruits. Grow in any fertile, well-drained soil.

1.5m / 1.5m

SPRING SUMMER AUTUMN WINTER

RUBUS FRUTICOSUS
BRAMBLE
ROSACEAE

Bramble is an excellent wildlife plant: larvae of the grizzled skipper and ringlet butterfly use it for food, bees, bumblebees and speckled wood butterflies feed on the nectar in its white flowers, and birds and small mammals eat the ripe blackberries. The dense branches create safe nesting sites. Any soil is suitable.

90cm / 3m

SPRING SUMMER AUTUMN WINTER

RUBUS IDAEUS
RASPBERRY
ROSACEAE

Raspberries are woodland plants that are usually confined to a fruit cage to prevent birds eating the fruit. Prickly arching stems are produced each year, and carry small flowers which are a good source of nectar for bees, followed by the typical deep red fruits. Small mammals also enjoy the fruit. Grow in well-drained soil.

1.8m / 1.8m

SPRING SUMMER AUTUMN WINTER

⬍ height and spread   ✳ feature of interest   ▢▢▢ season of interest   *SHRUBS* **P – R**

SHRUBS

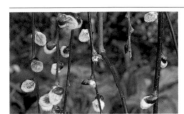

SALIX CAPREA
GOAT WILLOW
SALICACEAE

Goat willow is a joy in spring with its 'pussy willow' flowers which provide valuable early nectar and pollen for bees, bumblebees, butterflies, blue tits and blackcaps. It is happy in all but shallow chalk soils. The buds are eaten by marsh tits and coal tits and the seeds by many of the finches.

SALIX CINEREA
GREY SALLOW
SALICACEAE

This has long grey-green leaves and yellow catkins on the bare stems in early spring. Bees, bumblebees and butterflies seek out this early source of nectar. Sallows are the food plants for the larvae of the purple emperor and Camberwell beauty butterflies and several moths. It is very good in wet and moist soils.

SAMBUCUS NIGRA
ELDER
CAPRIFOLIACEAE

The clusters of scented creamy blossom in early summer attract many insects, which in turn attract insect-eating birds. The black elderberries are one of the first fruits to ripen and provide food for many garden birds. It grows in any soil, but prefers a moist, fertile one. An essential plant for the wild garden.

SKIMMIA JAPONICA
RUTACEAE

Skimmia makes a rounded dome of oval leathery dark green leaves, with clusters of white fragrant flowers in late spring and, on female bushes, clusters of red fruits in the autumn. To ensure fruiting there must be both male and female plants in a group. Bees take nectar and birds the fruit. Grow in fertile, well-drained, neutral to acid soils.

SYMPHORICARPOS ALBUS
SNOWBERRY
CAPRIFOLIACEAE

An invasive shrub with arching stems of round dull green leaves and tiny pink flowers, followed by round snow-white fruits. The nectar is very attractive to bees, bumblebees and wasps and the plant is used as an alternative food plant by the marsh fritillary butterfly. Birds eat the berries in autumn. Any soil is suitable.

SYRINGA VULGARIS
LILAC
OLEACEAE

Lilac is a popular spring-flowering shrub with a range of different coloured and double-flowered cultivars. The species has large cone-shaped flower heads of lilac-blue sweetly scented flowers which are attractive to insects seeking nectar. It will grow almost anywhere, but prefers full sun and a fertile, well-drained soil.

leaf type   light preference   speed of growth   ease of growth

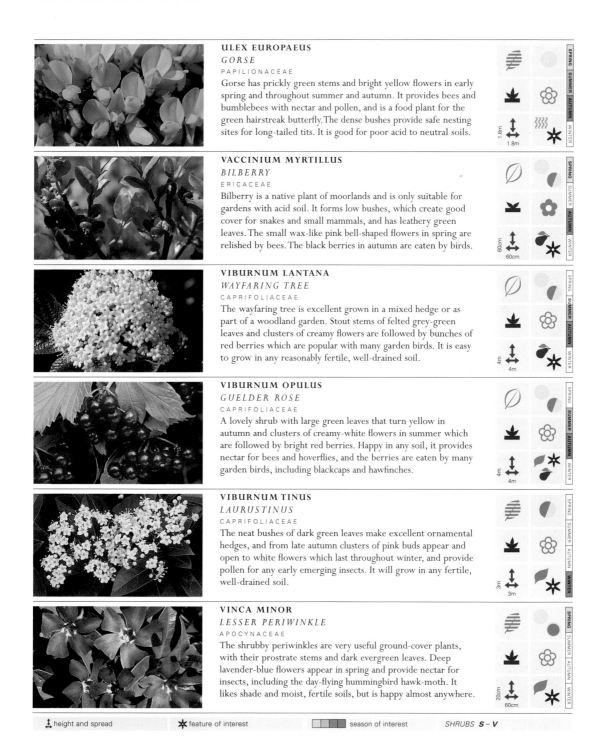

ULEX EUROPAEUS
GORSE
PAPILIONACEAE

Gorse has prickly green stems and bright yellow flowers in early spring and throughout summer and autumn. It provides bees and bumblebees with nectar and pollen, and is a food plant for the green hairstreak butterfly. The dense bushes provide safe nesting sites for long-tailed tits. It is good for poor acid to neutral soils.

VACCINIUM MYRTILLUS
BILBERRY
ERICACEAE

Bilberry is a native plant of moorlands and is only suitable for gardens with acid soil. It forms low bushes, which create good cover for snakes and small mammals, and has leathery green leaves. The small wax-like pink bell-shaped flowers in spring are relished by bees. The black berries in autumn are eaten by birds.

VIBURNUM LANTANA
WAYFARING TREE
CAPRIFOLIACEAE

The wayfaring tree is excellent grown in a mixed hedge or as part of a woodland garden. Stout stems of felted grey-green leaves and clusters of creamy flowers are followed by bunches of red berries which are popular with many garden birds. It is easy to grow in any reasonably fertile, well-drained soil.

VIBURNUM OPULUS
GUELDER ROSE
CAPRIFOLIACEAE

A lovely shrub with large green leaves that turn yellow in autumn and clusters of creamy-white flowers in summer which are followed by bright red berries. Happy in any soil, it provides nectar for bees and hoverflies, and the berries are eaten by many garden birds, including blackcaps and hawfinches.

VIBURNUM TINUS
LAURUSTINUS
CAPRIFOLIACEAE

The neat bushes of dark green leaves make excellent ornamental hedges, and from late autumn clusters of pink buds appear and open to white flowers which last throughout winter, and provide pollen for any early emerging insects. It will grow in any fertile, well-drained soil.

VINCA MINOR
LESSER PERIWINKLE
APOCYNACEAE

The shrubby periwinkles are very useful ground-cover plants, with their prostrate stems and dark evergreen leaves. Deep lavender-blue flowers appear in spring and provide nectar for insects, including the day-flying hummingbird hawk-moth. It likes shade and moist, fertile soils, but is happy almost anywhere.

height and spread   ✳ feature of interest   season of interest   *SHRUBS* **S – V**

CLIMBERS

CLEMATIS MONTANA
RANUNCULACEAE

One of the most attractive and vigorous ornamental climbers with white open flowers in late spring which smother the branches. The pink-flowered cultivars are more commonly seen in gardens covering pergolas and archways. Bees visit the flowers for pollen and birds nest in the twisting branches. It is good in any soil with adequate moisture.

CLEMATIS VITALBA
OLD MAN'S BEARD
RANUNCULACEAE

A native climber that decorates hedgerows with fluffy seedheads in autumn. The small white almond-scented flowers in summer are a popular source of nectar for bees, bumblebees, hoverflies and night-flying moths. Birds enjoy the seeds. It is unfussy, but prefers an alkaline soil. The plant can cause skin irritation.

HEDERA HELIX
IVY
ARALIACEAE

The flower buds provide food for the larvae of the holly blue butterfly, the sickly-scented, yellow-green flowers attract bees, small tortoiseshell butterflies and hoverflies to collect pollen and nectar and the black berries are eaten by many birds. All parts are poisonous. Any soil is suitable.

HUMULUS LUPULUS
HOP
CANNABACEAE

This perennial climber produces stems from the ground each year which twine around any support available and produce hop fruits on female plants. It succeeds in most fertile soils, and there is an attractive golden-leaved variety, 'Aureus'. It is one of the food plants for the larvae of the comma butterfly.

JASMINUM OFFICINALE
JASMINE
OLEACEAE

Jasmine is a vigorous woody climber whose twining stems produce attractive green leaves, evergreen in all but the coldest winters. Small clusters of very fragrant white star-like flowers are borne throughout summer. The flowers attract moths for nectar in the evening. It prefers moist, fertile soil.

LATHYRUS LATIFOLIUS
EVERLASTING PEA
PAPILIONACEAE

A perennial climber which dies back in winter but grows vigorously each spring. The greenish stems bear pairs of grey-green leaves and rose-pink pea-like flowers, throughout summer and into autumn, which attract bees. It is a food plant for the larvae of the long-tailed blue butterfly. It prefers a fertile soil.

---

leaf type light preference speed of growth ease of growth

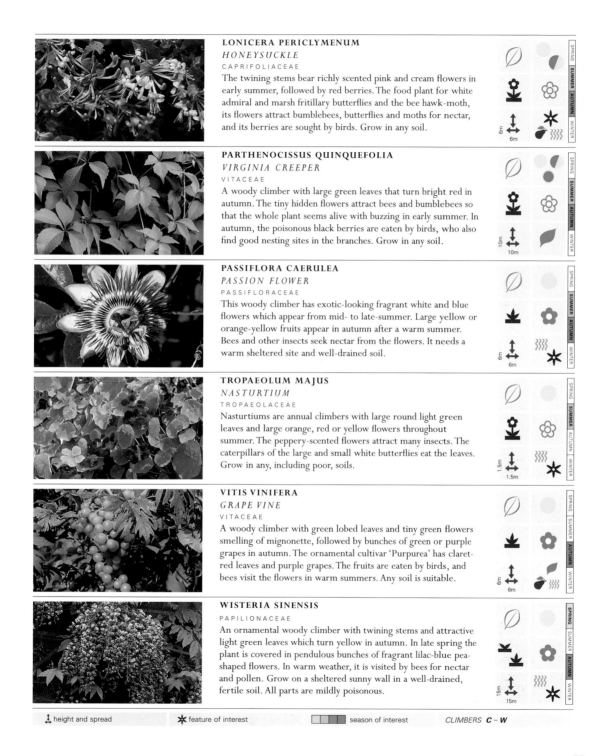

LONICERA PERICLYMENUM
HONEYSUCKLE
CAPRIFOLIACEAE

The twining stems bear richly scented pink and cream flowers in early summer, followed by red berries. The food plant for white admiral and marsh fritillary butterflies and the bee hawk-moth, its flowers attract bumblebees, butterflies and moths for nectar, and its berries are sought by birds. Grow in any soil.

PARTHENOCISSUS QUINQUEFOLIA
VIRGINIA CREEPER
VITACEAE

A woody climber with large green leaves that turn bright red in autumn. The tiny hidden flowers attract bees and bumblebees so that the whole plant seems alive with buzzing in early summer. In autumn, the poisonous black berries are eaten by birds, who also find good nesting sites in the branches. Grow in any soil.

PASSIFLORA CAERULEA
PASSION FLOWER
PASSIFLORACEAE

This woody climber has exotic-looking fragrant white and blue flowers which appear from mid- to late-summer. Large yellow or orange-yellow fruits appear in autumn after a warm summer. Bees and other insects seek nectar from the flowers. It needs a warm sheltered site and well-drained soil.

TROPAEOLUM MAJUS
NASTURTIUM
TROPAEOLACEAE

Nasturtiums are annual climbers with large round light green leaves and large orange, red or yellow flowers throughout summer. The peppery-scented flowers attract many insects. The caterpillars of the large and small white butterflies eat the leaves. Grow in any, including poor, soils.

VITIS VINIFERA
GRAPE VINE
VITACEAE

A woody climber with green lobed leaves and tiny green flowers smelling of mignonette, followed by bunches of green or purple grapes in autumn. The ornamental cultivar 'Purpurea' has claret-red leaves and purple grapes. The fruits are eaten by birds, and bees visit the flowers in warm summers. Any soil is suitable.

WISTERIA SINENSIS
PAPILIONACEAE

An ornamental woody climber with twining stems and attractive light green leaves which turn yellow in autumn. In late spring the plant is covered in pendulous bunches of fragrant lilac-blue pea-shaped flowers. In warm weather, it is visited by bees for nectar and pollen. Grow on a sheltered sunny wall in a well-drained, fertile soil. All parts are mildly poisonous.

height and spread   feature of interest   season of interest   *CLIMBERS* **C – W**

TREES

ACER CAMPESTRE
FIELD MAPLE
ACERACEAE
The field maple is usually found in hedgerows but eventually makes a most attractive round-headed specimen with lobed leaves which turn yellow and apricot in autumn as the winged seeds ripen. The small green flowers produce nectar and pollen for bees and other insects. It tolerates most well-drained soils.

ACER PSEUDOPLATANUS
SYCAMORE
ACERACEAE
A tree often considered a nuisance but still a valuable resource for wildlife. The large leaves provide food for many insects, and the small light green flowers provide useful early nectar and pollen for both bees and bumblebees. The winged seeds are eaten by tits and chaffinches. Any soil is suitable.

AESCULUS HIPPOCASTANUM
HORSE CHESTNUT
HIPPOCASTANACEAE
A statuesque tree with large palmate leaves opening from the typical 'sticky' buds in early spring. Large upright cones of white flowers ornament the tree in late spring and are followed by 'conkers' in autumn. Bees and bumblebees visit the flowers for nectar and the pollen. Deep, fertile soil is required.

ALNUS GLUTINOSA
ALDER
BETULACEAE
The alder has rounded leaves and male catkins in early spring which are much sought after for pollen by bees and bumblebees. The female flowers ripen into cone-like fruits which provide food for reed buntings and marsh tits. Host to 90 insects, it is tolerant of most conditions, particularly pollution and wet soils.

AMELANCHIER LAMARCKII
SNOWY MESPILUS
ROSACEAE
An attractive small tree, with starry white flowers in late spring and light green leaves which turn orange and red in autumn. After a warm summer, fruits appear in autumn, which are popular with a range of birds such as warblers, thrushes and jays. It tolerates almost any soil but prefers it slightly moist.

BETULA PENDULA
BIRCH
BETULACEAE
The silver birch is an elegant tree with white bark, pendulous green leaves and male catkins in spring. In autumn the seeds are eaten by many birds. The older trunks make ideal nesting holes and the tree is host to over 200 insects including the orange underwing moth. It is tolerant of all but wet soils.

leaf type   light preference   speed of growth   ease of growth

CARPINUS BETULUS
HORNBEAM
CORYLACEAE

Hornbeam is normally found in hedgerows but will make a large rounded-head tree excellent for formal hedges or pleaching, with leaves like those of the beech. Host to over 30 insects, it produces nutlets in autumn which are eaten by jays, nuthatches and finches. It is tolerant of almost all soils, including heavy clay.

18m
18m

CASTANEA SATIVA
SWEET CHESTNUT
FAGACEAE

The sweet chestnut is found in woodlands and has long, coarsely toothed leaves and yellow catkins in summer, followed by prickly-coated fruits that open to disclose shiny brown chestnuts. Bees visit the flowers for pollen and nectar and birds eat the seeds. It prefers a rich, deep loam soil.

18m
18m

CATALPA BIGNONIOIDES
INDIAN BEAN TREE
BIGNONIACEAE

An attractive tree with large leaves which turn yellow in autumn and provide plenty of shade. The fragrant white flowers, carried in upright panicles in summer, are followed by long hanging bean-shaped fruits. Large numbers of bees and bumblebees visit the flowers for nectar and pollen. It prefers a deep, rich soil.

12m
12m

CERCIS SILIQUASTRUM
JUDAS TREE
CAESALPINIACEAE

A small tree with purple-rose flowers carried on the branches in late spring just before the leaves appear. The flowers are visited freely by bees for nectar and pollen. The blue-green leaves turn yellow in autumn when grey-green pods hang down from the branches. It prefers a well-drained, neutral to acid soil.

6m
6m

CRATAEGUS MONOGYNA
HAWTHORN
ROSACEAE

Hawthorn is one of the major constituents of hedgerows. It tolerates almost any conditions including polluted and exposed sites. The honey-scented white blossom is followed by clusters of red fruits (haws) which are eaten by birds and mice. The hawthorn provides food for over 150 insects.

6m
6m

FAGUS SYLVATICA
BEECH
FAGACEAE

Beech has round shiny green leaves which remain on hedge plants throughout winter. It is host to 60 insects, including the lobster moth, and the beech nuts produced in autumn are food for birds, squirrels and small mammals. The seeds are mildly poisonous. Grow in any well-drained soil.

30m
30m

 height and spread   ✱ feature of interest   ▢▢▢▨ season of interest   *TREES* **A – F**

99

TREES

FRAXINUS EXCELSIOR
ASH
OLEACEAE

Tolerant of a wide range of soil and conditions, ash is a common tree in copses and woodland. Its leaves arrive late and fall early which restricts its garden use but it is host to 40 insects, including the privet hawk-moth. The winged seeds are eaten by many birds including woodpeckers.

JUGLANS REGIA
WALNUT
JUGLANDACEAE

The walnut has large leaves and round green fruits in autumn containing the familiar walnut. It is only a useful tree for wildlife if a good fruiting cultivar like 'Broadview' is selected. Nuts are eaten by several birds, including jackdaws and hawfinches, as well as squirrels. Any well-drained fertile soil is suitable.

LARIX DECIDUA
LARCH
PINACEAE

A deciduous conifer which is tolerant of a wide range of conditions and soils. The tufts of bright green needles turn yellow in autumn when the brown female cones shed their seeds. Crossbills prise open the cones to get at the seeds, and the seeds also provide food for tits, nuthatches and finches.

MALUS DOMESTICA
APPLE
ROSACEAE

Apple trees in blossom provide a valuable source of late-spring nectar and pollen for honeybees. Many insects feed on the foliage, flowers and fruits, often causing a problem for fruit-growers. Ripe apples left on the ground provide food for butterflies, birds and small mammals. Well-drained soil is needed.

MALUS SYLVESTRIS
CRAB APPLE
ROSACEAE

This has pink-tinged white flowers in spring, followed by small red crab apples in autumn. It is host to 90 insects and a source of nectar and pollen for bees and bumblebees. Birds and mice enjoy the fruits. The cultivated crab apples are more attractive and almost as good for wildlife. Any well-drained soil is suitable.

MORUS NIGRA
BLACK MULBERRY
MORACEAE

The white mulberry, *M. alba*, has white fruit and leaves which are used for feeding silkworms, and the black mulberry has delicious juicy black fruits and darker leaves. The fruits are very popular with many birds. Best grown in a rich, moist soil, the trees may need support as they age.

leaf type · light preference · speed of growth · ease of growth

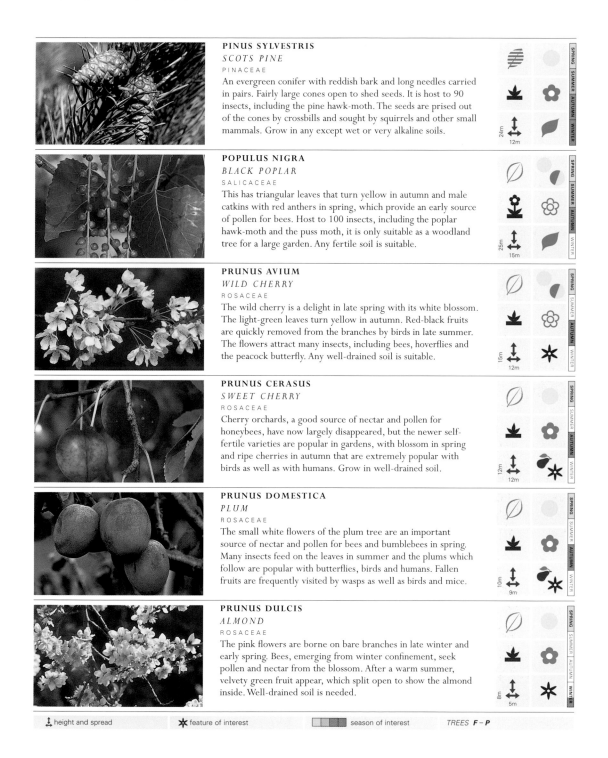

PINUS SYLVESTRIS
SCOTS PINE
PINACEAE

An evergreen conifer with reddish bark and long needles carried in pairs. Fairly large cones open to shed seeds. It is host to 90 insects, including the pine hawk-moth. The seeds are prised out of the cones by crossbills and sought by squirrels and other small mammals. Grow in any except wet or very alkaline soils.

24m
12m

SPRING SUMMER AUTUMN WINTER

POPULUS NIGRA
BLACK POPLAR
SALICACEAE

This has triangular leaves that turn yellow in autumn and male catkins with red anthers in spring, which provide an early source of pollen for bees. Host to 100 insects, including the poplar hawk-moth and the puss moth, it is only suitable as a woodland tree for a large garden. Any fertile soil is suitable.

25m
15m

SPRING SUMMER AUTUMN WINTER

PRUNUS AVIUM
WILD CHERRY
ROSACEAE

The wild cherry is a delight in late spring with its white blossom. The light-green leaves turn yellow in autumn. Red-black fruits are quickly removed from the branches by birds in late summer. The flowers attract many insects, including bees, hoverflies and the peacock butterfly. Any well-drained soil is suitable.

15m
12m

SPRING SUMMER AUTUMN WINTER

PRUNUS CERASUS
SWEET CHERRY
ROSACEAE

Cherry orchards, a good source of nectar and pollen for honeybees, have now largely disappeared, but the newer self-fertile varieties are popular in gardens, with blossom in spring and ripe cherries in autumn that are extremely popular with birds as well as with humans. Grow in well-drained soil.

12m
12m

SPRING SUMMER AUTUMN WINTER

PRUNUS DOMESTICA
PLUM
ROSACEAE

The small white flowers of the plum tree are an important source of nectar and pollen for bees and bumblebees in spring. Many insects feed on the leaves in summer and the plums which follow are popular with butterflies, birds and humans. Fallen fruits are frequently visited by wasps as well as birds and mice.

10m
9m

SPRING SUMMER AUTUMN WINTER

PRUNUS DULCIS
ALMOND
ROSACEAE

The pink flowers are borne on bare branches in late winter and early spring. Bees, emerging from winter confinement, seek pollen and nectar from the blossom. After a warm summer, velvety green fruit appear, which split open to show the almond inside. Well-drained soil is needed.

8m
5m

SPRING SUMMER AUTUMN WINTER

↕ height and spread   ✱ feature of interest   ▢▢▢▢ season of interest   *TREES* **F – P**

TREES

PRUNUS PADUS
BIRD CHERRY
ROSACEAE
The bird cherry carries scented white blossoms in late spring, which are popular with many insects, including bees and bumblebees, and with bullfinches. The black bitter cherries in late summer are enjoyed by many birds, including blackbirds. Any well-drained soil is suitable.

PRUNUS SPINOSA
SLOE
ROSACEAE
This tree has vicious thorns and clouds of small white blossom in early spring, which provide nectar and pollen for bees and bumblebees. It is a host plant for larvae of the black and brown hairstreak butterflies as well as the emperor moth. Black 'sloes' appear in autumn and are eaten by birds. Any soil is suitable.

PYRUS COMMUNIS
WILD PEAR
ROSACEAE
The wild pear produces clouds of pink-tinged white blossom in spring, followed by edible green fruits in late summer and autumn. Bees visit the blossoms for nectar and pollen, as do numerous other insects. Birds, butterflies and small mammals feed on the ripe fruits. It prefers a fertile soil.

PYRUS COMMUNIS 'CONFERENCE'
CONFERENCE PEAR
ROSACEAE
'Conference' is one of the easiest cultivated pears to grow, being self-fertile. Clusters of white blossom in mid-spring are followed by green pears in autumn. The blossom is visited by bees and bumblebees and the ripe fruits by butterflies and birds. Windfalls are popular with small mammals. Grow in any fertile soil.

QUERCUS ROBUR
OAK
FAGACEAE
A tree of woods and parkland which is host to around 300 types of insect. The catkin flowers appear in early spring before the lobed leaves, and acorns are produced in large quantities in autumn. Nuthatches and jays feed on the acorns, as do squirrels, dormice and other small mammals. Any soil is suitable.

ROBINIA PSEUDOACACIA
FALSE ACACIA
PAPILIONACEAE
The false acacia has light green leaves and scented white pea-shaped flowers in early summer, which are visited by bees for pollen and nectar. There is a golden-leaved cultivar 'Frisia', which is less vigorous. It is tolerant of most well-drained conditions and good on dry, sandy soils.

| 🍃 leaf type | ⬤ light preference | ⚲ speed of growth | ⚙ ease of growth |

SALIX ALBA
WHITE WILLOW
SALICACEAE

The white willow has long leaves covered in silky white hairs, and produces pale yellow catkins in early spring. There are garden cultivars with coloured stems. The host plant to 250 insects, it provides bees and bumblebees with nectar and pollen. Birds feed on the insects. Any, even waterlogged, soil is suitable.

15m / 15m

SORBUS ARIA
WHITEBEAM
ROSACEAE

The whitebeam is an attractive tree with large ribbed leaves, which turn yellow in autumn, and clusters of white flowers in late spring which are visited by many insects. Large clusters of red berries are produced in autumn, which are eaten by many garden birds. Any well-drained soil is suitable.

12m / 8m

SORBUS AUCUPARIA
ROWAN
ROSACEAE

Host to 30 insects, the rowan has fluffy white flowers in early summer which are popular with bees, and the clusters of red berries in autumn are devoured by many birds, including blackbirds and fieldfares, and small mammals. The rowan tolerates most soils, but grows best in well-drained acid soil.

12m / 8m

TAXUS BACCATA
YEW
TAXACEAE

The yew has dark evergreen needles, and is a valuable hedging plant for the garden which provides good nesting sites for birds. The red autumn fruits are popular with many birds, including robins, mistle thrushes, and greenfinches. All parts are poisonous. It is tolerant of all except extremely acid soils.

12m / 15m

TILIA CORDATA
LIME
TILIACEAE

The small-leaved lime has pointed round leaves that are smaller than in other limes, but it shares the same bunches of small scented dull white flowers, an important source of nectar for both honey- and bumblebees. It is host to 30 insects, and the seeds are eaten by finches. Grow in a deep, fertile, alkaline soil.

30m / 20m

ULMUS GLABRA
WYCH ELM
ULMACEAE

The wych elm can still be found in hedgerows, its red-tinged tiny flowers providing pollen for bees in early spring. It is the food plant for the larvae of the large tortoiseshell and white hairstreak butterflies. The seeds are eaten by greenfinches. It prefers a rich, deep, fertile soil.

30m / 24m

SPRING SUMMER AUTUMN WINTER

↕ height and spread   ✳ feature of interest   season of interest   *TREES* **P – U**

HERBS

ALLIUM SCHOENOPRASUM
CHIVES
ALLIACEAE

Chives are a useful culinary herb, their leaves adding flavour to soups, omelettes and salads. The round pale purple flower heads can also be used in salads, and are visited by bees and butterflies for nectar. Chives are a good edging plant and prefer a rich, moist but well-drained soil.

ALLIUM URSINUM
WILD GARLIC
ALLIACEAE

Wild garlic has large shiny leaves which give off a garlic scent when crushed, and can be used to flavour salads and soups. The round white flower heads in spring and summer are visited by a wide range of insects, including bees and wasps. Grow from seed sown where it is to grow, in a moist fertile soil.

ANGELICA ARCHANGELICA
ANGELICA
APIACEAE

Angelica is an elegant biennial which has large aromatic toothed leaves, strong hollow stems and large round clusters of scented greenish-white flowers in summer. Large numbers of insects are attracted to the flowers which in turn attract insect-eating birds. It prefers a rich, moist soil.

BORAGO OFFICINALIS
BORAGE
BORAGINACEAE

An attractive annual with hairy stems, leaves tasting of cucumber, and sky-blue edible flowers with black cone-like centres, borage is one of the best herbs to attract bees and bumblebees for nectar. Easy to grow from seed, it will self-seed in the garden and come up year after year. Any well-drained soil is suitable.

FOENICULUM VULGARE
FENNEL
APIACEAE

Fennel is a vigorous perennial which will readily self-seed. The tall stems carry very fine aromatic leaves and large clusters of small yellow flowers, which attract insects including bees, wasps and hoverflies. The leaves are eaten by the larvae of the swallowtail butterfly. A well-drained soil is preferable.

HYSSOPUS OFFICINALIS
HYSSOP
LAMIACEAE

Hyssop has long been grown for its therapeutic uses. The neat round bushes produce small aromatic dark green leaves and short spikes of blue flowers throughout summer and into autumn. The flowers are a source of both pollen and nectar for bees and are popular with lacewings and butterflies. It needs well-drained soil.

 leaf type   light preference   speed of growth   ease of growth

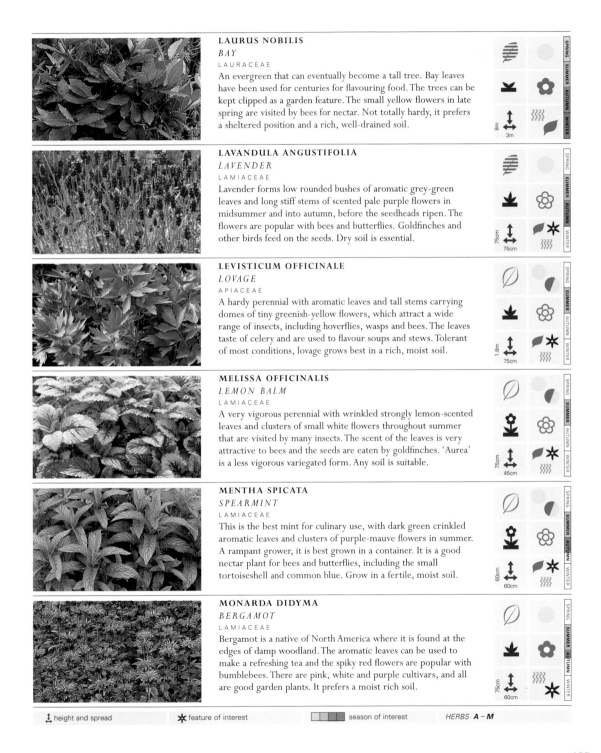

LAURUS NOBILIS
BAY
LAURACEAE
An evergreen that can eventually become a tall tree. Bay leaves have been used for centuries for flavouring food. The trees can be kept clipped as a garden feature. The small yellow flowers in late spring are visited by bees for nectar. Not totally hardy, it prefers a sheltered position and a rich, well-drained soil.

LAVANDULA ANGUSTIFOLIA
LAVENDER
LAMIACEAE
Lavender forms low rounded bushes of aromatic grey-green leaves and long stiff stems of scented pale purple flowers in midsummer and into autumn, before the seedheads ripen. The flowers are popular with bees and butterflies. Goldfinches and other birds feed on the seeds. Dry soil is essential.

LEVISTICUM OFFICINALE
LOVAGE
APIACEAE
A hardy perennial with aromatic leaves and tall stems carrying domes of tiny greenish-yellow flowers, which attract a wide range of insects, including hoverflies, wasps and bees. The leaves taste of celery and are used to flavour soups and stews. Tolerant of most conditions, lovage grows best in a rich, moist soil.

MELISSA OFFICINALIS
LEMON BALM
LAMIACEAE
A very vigorous perennial with wrinkled strongly lemon-scented leaves and clusters of small white flowers throughout summer that are visited by many insects. The scent of the leaves is very attractive to bees and the seeds are eaten by goldfinches. 'Aurea' is a less vigorous variegated form. Any soil is suitable.

MENTHA SPICATA
SPEARMINT
LAMIACEAE
This is the best mint for culinary use, with dark green crinkled aromatic leaves and clusters of purple-mauve flowers in summer. A rampant grower, it is best grown in a container. It is a good nectar plant for bees and butterflies, including the small tortoiseshell and common blue. Grow in a fertile, moist soil.

MONARDA DIDYMA
BERGAMOT
LAMIACEAE
Bergamot is a native of North America where it is found at the edges of damp woodland. The aromatic leaves can be used to make a refreshing tea and the spiky red flowers are popular with bumblebees. There are pink, white and purple cultivars, and all are good garden plants. It prefers a moist rich soil.

↕ height and spread   ✳ feature of interest   ▭ season of interest   *HERBS **A – M***

HERBS

MYRRHIS ODORATA
SWEET CICELY
APIACEAE

With elegant feathery leaves and large fluffy white flower heads in early summer, this makes an attractive addition to any garden. The whole plant is aniseed-scented and has long been used as a natural sweetener for stewed fruit. The flowers are popular with bees and other insects. Almost any soil is suitable.

NEPETA CATARIA
CATNIP
LAMIACEAE

Catnip has serrated aromatic leaves and clusters of white flowers which appear throughout summer. Traditionally used in herbal medicine, its main use today is as a stuffing for cat toys. The flowers attract bees and butterflies for nectar. Grow in any dry or well-drained garden soil.

OCIMUM BASILICUM
BASIL
LAMIACEAE

A tender plant grown as an annual, with bright green shiny strongly scented leaves and clusters of white flowers in summer which are popular with bees seeking nectar. It is an essential culinary herb for flavouring salads and tomato dishes. Plant out in midsummer in well-drained soil and a warm position.

ORIGANUM VULGARE
MARJORAM
LAMIACEAE

There are lots of cultivated marjorams but this is one of the best for culinary use. Domes of soft hairy aromatic evergreen leaves are covered in round flower heads of tiny mauve flowers in summer. It is one of the very best bee and butterfly plants. Any well-drained soil is suitable.

ROSMARINUS OFFICINALIS
ROSEMARY
LAMIACEAE

An upright shrub with evergreen aromatic leaves and pale blue flowers in late spring, but also intermittently throughout the year, rosemary is an essential plant for any herb garden. The flowers are very attractive to bees, hoverflies and to the occasional butterfly. It needs shelter and a well-drained soil.

SALVIA OFFICINALIS
SAGE
LAMIACEAE

Sage is an evergreen shrub with large oval aromatic dark-green leaves. In summer it bears upright stems of mauve-blue flowers which are visited by bees for nectar. There are several very attractive cultivars including 'Icterina' and 'Purpurascens'. It needs a warm, well-drained, alkaline soil.

| leaf type | light preference | speed of growth | ease of growth |

SAPONARIA OFFICINALIS
SOAPWORT

CARYOPHYLLACEAE

The leaves and root of soapwort were traditionally used for washing delicate fabrics. It has showy pink flowers and attractive smooth green leaves. The sweetly scented flowers are visited by moths in the evening. There are double-flowered forms available, and all prefer a damp, fertile soil.

75cm / 45cm

SATUREJA MONTANA
WINTER SAVORY

LAMIACEAE

Winter savory is a semi-evergreen sub-shrub which forms neat domes of small aromatic dark green leaves and small white flowers throughout summer which are extremely attractive to bees. The peppery-flavoured leaves are used to add seasoning to cooked vegetables. It prefers a poor, dry soil.

30cm / 45cm

SYMPHYTUM OFFICINALE
COMFREY

BORAGINACEAE

Comfrey has large rough leaves and delicate sprays of nodding cream or purple flowers. The flowers are visited by bees and bumblebees for pollen and nectar, and the leaves are eaten by moth and butterfly larvae. Happy in most moist soils, including heavy clay, comfrey can become invasive.

90cm / 90cm

TANACETUM VULGARE
TANSY

ASTERACEAE

Long used as a herb for flavouring and as an insect repellent, tansy has dark green lacy foliage and tall stems of small yellow flower heads. It can be very invasive, so remove the dead flowers before they set seed. The flowers are attractive to bees, bumblebees and butterflies. It grows in any well-drained soil.

1.2m / 90cm

THYMUS POLYTRICHUS SUBSP. BRITANNICUS
CREEPING THYME

LAMIACEAE

This is found on dry banks and heaths, with creeping stems of tiny aromatic green leaves and round heads of pale mauve flowers which are very popular with bees and bumblebees seeking nectar and pollen. Used traditionally in herbal medicine, it is ideal for planting between paving. It needs very well-drained conditions.

5cm / 20cm

THYMUS VULGARIS
THYME

LAMIACEAE

There are many types of thyme but this is the best, forming low domes of tiny aromatic leaves covered in round heads of tiny mauve flowers in summer which are continuously visited by bees, bumblebees and butterflies seeking nectar. It needs a sheltered site and a poor, well-drained or even dry soil.

30cm / 30cm

---

height and spread   feature of interest   season of interest   *HERBS* **M – T**

GLOSSARY

ALPINE: A plant that in its natural mountain habitat grows above the uppermost limit of trees. More colloquially, plants that are suitable for rock gardens are called alpines.

ANNUAL: A plant that grows from seed, flowers and dies within the same year. Some half-hardy perennial plants are used as annuals, that is, they die off in the winter.

AQUATIC PLANT: A plant that lives totally or partly submerged in water.

BEDDING PLANTS: Plants that are set out for a temporary seasonal displays and discarded at the end of the season.

BIENNIAL: A plant raised from seed that makes its initial growth in one year and flowers during the following one, then dies.

BOG GARDEN PLANTS: Plants that live with their roots in moist soil.

BULB: An underground food storage organ formed of fleshy, modified leaves that enclose a dormant shoot.

CALYX: The outer and protective part of a flower. It is usually green and is very apparent in roses.

COMPOST: Vegetable waste from kitchens, as well as soft parts of garden plants, which is encouraged to decompose and to form a material that can be dug into soil or used to create a mulch around plants.

CORM: An underground storage organ formed of a swollen stem base, for example, a gladiolus.

CULTIVAR: A shortened term for 'cultivated variety' that indicates a variety raised in cultivation. Strictly speaking, most modern varieties are cultivars, but the term 'variety' is still widely used because it is familiar to most gardeners.

CUTTING: A section of plant which is detached and encouraged to form roots and stems to provide a new independent plant. Cuttings may be taken from roots, stems or leaves.

DEAD-HEADING: The removal of a faded flower head to prevent the formation of seeds and to encourage the development of further flowers.

DECIDUOUS: Plants that lose their leaves during the winter are referred to as deciduous.

DORMANT: When a plant is alive but is making no growth, it is called dormant. The dormant period is usually the winter.

EVERGREEN: Plants that appear to be green throughout the year and not to lose their leaves are called evergreen. In reality, however, they shed some of their leaves throughout the year, while producing others.

FRIABLE: Soil that is crumbly and light and easily worked. The term especially applies to soil being prepared as a seedbed in spring.

HALF-HARDY: A plant that can withstand fairly low temperatures, but needs protection from frost.

HALF-HARDY ANNUAL: An annual that is sown in gentle warmth in a greenhouse in spring, the seedlings being transferred to wider spacings in pots or boxes. The plants are placed in a garden or container only when all risk of frost has passed.

HARDEN OFF: To gradually accustom plants to cooler conditions so that they can be planted outside.

HARDY: A plant that is able to survive outdoors in winter. In the case of some rock-garden plants, good drainage is essential to ensure their survival.

HERB: A plant that is grown for its aromatic qualities and can often be used in cooking or medicinally.

HERBACEOUS PERENNIAL: A plant with no woody tissue that lives for several years. It may be deciduous or evergreen.

HYBRID: A cross between two different species, varieties or genera of plants.

LOAM: Friable mixture of sand, silt and clay.

MARGINAL PLANTS: Plants that live in shallow water at the edges of ponds. Some also thrive in boggy soil surrounding a pond.

MULCHING: Covering the soil around plants with well-decayed organic material such as garden compost, peat or, in the case of rock garden plants, stone chippings or 6mm (¼in) shingle.

NEUTRAL: Soil that is neither acid nor alkaline, with a pH of 7.0, is said to be neutral. Most plants grow in a pH of about 6.5.

PEAT: A naturally occurring substance formed from partly rotted organic material in waterlogged soils, used as a growing medium and soil additive.

PERENNIAL: Any plant that lives for three or more years is called a perennial.

PERGOLA: An open timber structure made up of linked arches.

PLEACHING: Twining or interlacing the branches of a shrub or tree to form a hedge.

POTTING COMPOST: Traditionally, a compost formed of loam, sharp sand and peat, fertilizers and chalk. The ratio of the ingredients is altered according to whether the compost is used for sowing seeds, potting-up or repotting plants into larger containers. Recognition of the environmental importance of conserving peat beds has led to many modern composts being formed of other organic materials, such as coir or shredded bark.

PRICKING OUT: Transplanting seedlings from the container in which they were sown to one where they are more widely spaced.

RAISED BED: A raised area that is encircled by a wall or other barrier. Rock garden plants can be grown both in the raised bed and the wall.

RHIZOME: An underground or partly buried horizontal stem. They can be slender or fleshy. Some irises have thick, fleshy rhizomes, while those of lily-of-the-valley are slender and creeping. They act as storage organs and perpetuate plants from one season to another.

SCREE BED: An area formed of layers of rubble, gravel, and compost, imitating naturally occurring scree.

SEED LEAVES: The first leaves that develop on a seedling, which are coarser and more robust than the true leaves.

SEMI-EVERGREEN: A plant that may keep all or some of its leaves in a reasonably mild winter.

SINK GARDENS: Old stone sinks partly filled with drainage material and then with freely draining compost. They are planted with miniature conifers and bulbs, as well as small rock garden plants. These features are usually displayed on terraces and patios.

SPECIES ROSE: A common term for a wild rose or one of its near relatives.

STAMEN: The male part of a flower, comprising the filament (stalk) and the anthers, which contain pollen.

STANDARD: A tree or shrub trained to form a rounded head of branches at the top of a clear stem.

STIGMA: The tip of the female part of a flower. It is the part on which pollen alights.

SUB-SHRUB: Small and spreading shrub with a woody base. It differs from normal shrubs in that when grown in temperate regions its upper stems and shoots die back during winter.

TILTH: Friable topsoil in which seeds are sown. It also acts as a mulch on the surface of soil, helping to reduce the loss of moisture from the soil's surface.

TOPSOIL: The uppermost layer of soil that is structured and contains organic matter and humus.

TUBER: A swollen, thickened and fleshy stem or root. Some tubers are swollen roots (dahlia), while others are swollen stems (potato). They serve as storage organs and help to perpetuate plants from one season to another.

VARIEGATED: Usually applied to leaves and used to describe a state of having two or more colours.

VARIETY: A naturally occurring variation of a species that retains its characteristics when propagated. The term is often used for cultivars.

WILDLIFE POND: An informal pond that encourages the presence of wildlife such as frogs, birds, insects and small mammals.

INDEX

ACKNOWLEDGEMENTS

t *top* **b** *below* **l** *left* **r** *right* ***Directory a–f**, starting from top*

A-Z Botanical Collection 71d / Pam Collins 67d / Anthony Cooper 103e /
Mike Danson 77c, 78d / Derrick Ditchburn 72f / F.Merlet 75e / Maurice Nimmo 79b /
Annie Poole 76f / T.G.J.Rayner 73d / Derek Shimmin 82a / Roger Standen 70e /
Jan Staples 69b, f, 76c/ John Stiles 106a / Bjorn Svensson 72c;

Bruce Coleman Collection / John Cancalosi, 35l / Dennis Green 29l / Robert Maier 17 /
George McCarthy 56 / Andrew Purcell 34r / Marie Read 28r / Hans Reinhard 18t;

Liz Eddison 2 & 22, 7, 14b, 19, 24, 38, 40, 48, 58–59, 87d / John Chambers 54 /
Carol Klein, Chelsea '99 10–11, 12t;

The Garden Picture Library 33r / Chris Burrows 32l / Brian Carter 6, 16t, 28l, 29r, 32r /
Kathy Charlton 4 & 33l / Geoff Dann 63b / David England 78f / John Glover 30r, 71e /
Sunniva Harte 35r / Neil Holmes 83c / Andrea Jones 16b & 112 / Jerry Pavia 73b, e;

John Glover 1 & 30l, 5, 12b, 13, 14t, 18b, 20, 31l, r, 34l, 37, 42, 44, 46, 52 /
Gavin Diarmuid, Chelsea '95 15 / Marnie Hall, Chelsea '98 50 / Marnie Smith 25–26;

Peter McHoy 62a, 63d, 64a, c, 65b, c, 66d, 67c, 68a, c, 70b, 74e, 77d, 78b, e, 79a, 81a, f, 83a,
84e, f, 86b, e, 87b, 89a, b, 90a, d, 92e, 93b, 94a, f, 95e, 97c, e, f, 98e, 99a, b, f, 100a, d, 102c,
103b, f, 105b, d, 106e, f;

The Harry Smith Collection 62b,c,d,e,f, 63a,c,e,f, 64b,e,f, 65a,d,e,f, 66a,b,c,e,f, 67a,b,e,f,
68b,d,e,f, 69a,c,d,e, 70a,c,d,f, 71a,b,c,f, 72a,b,d,e, 73a,c,f, 74a,b,c,d,f, 75a,b,c,d,f, 76a,b,d,e,
77a,b,f, 78a,c, 79c,d,e,f, 80a,b,c,d,e,f, 81b,c,d, 82b,c,d,e,f, 83b,d,e,f, 84a,b,c,d, 85a,b,c,d,e,f,
86a,c,d,f, 87a,c,e,f, 88a,b,c,d,e,f, 89c,d,f, 90b,c,e,f, 91b,c,d,e,f, 92a,b,c,d,f, 93a,c,d,e,f,
94b,c,d,e, 95a,b,c,d,f, 96a,b,c,d,e,f, 97a,b,d, 98a,b,c,d, 99c,d,e, 100b,c,e,f, 101a,b,c,d,e,f,
102a,b,d,e,f, 103a,c,d, 104a,b,c,d,f, 105a,c,e,f, 106b,c,d, 107a,b,c,d,e,f;

David Squire 64d, 77e, 81e, 89e, 91a, 98f, 104e.